"A step-by-st⟨...⟩
hensive yet co⟨...⟩
electronic de⟨...⟩
time-tested tr⟨...⟩
day-by-day. I w⟨...⟩ ⟨...⟩ by the plain yet prudent
recommendation to pray with a book, not an app!
This is a timely book for a fast-paced age."

—JOHN CHRYSSAVGIS, author of *John: Desert Wisdom for Everyday Life*

"Vassa Larin makes brilliant observations about
how technologies of measuring time change the
way we perceive it. Thus, transition from sundial
to mechanical clock became a major revolution
that has shaped modernity. Social media again
revolutionized our experience of time. She suggests
liturgical circles, with focus on the service of hours,
to make our time prayable and livable again."

—CYRIL HOVORUN, author of *Scaffolds of the Church: Towards Posstructural Ecclesiology*

"This is indeed a timely book. Sr. Vassa Larin guides
us in a knowledgeable, yet also personal and practical way, into the mystery of time as it is embodied in
the cycles of liturgical time in the Orthodox tradition. The vision offered here, and her suggestions for
living this tradition, open a way for each reader to
'redeem the time,' as exhorted by the Apostle."

—JOHN BEHR, author of *John the Theologian and His Paschal Gospel: A Prologue to Theology*

"In this wonderful book, Sister Vassa Larin introduces us to the practice of praying the 'Little' Hours of Byzantine Daily Prayer, that is, the First (Prime), Third (Terce), Sixth (Sext) and Ninth (None) hours, so often neglected in contemporary usage. More than a beautiful commentary on these particular hours, Larin offers us here a rich theology of the church 'redeeming the time' through prayer. This is a must read not only for Orthodox Christians but for all of us."

—MAXWELL E. JOHNSON, professor of theology, University of Notre Dame

"We live in an age in which time has been flattened out and proceeds relentlessly—24/7. Sister Vassa Larin draws on the wisdom enshrined in the prayer offices of the Orthodox Church to enable us to mark the hours of the day and mark the days of the week. In this way we shall discern the rhythms and cycles of time and thus learn to redeem it."

—ANDREW LOUTH, professor emeritus, Durham University

Praying in Time

Praying in Time

The Hours & Days in Step with Orthodox Christian Tradition

VASSA LARIN

WIPF & STOCK · Eugene, Oregon

PRAYING IN TIME
The Hours & Days in Step with Orthodox Christian Tradition

Wipf & Stock
An Imprint of Wipf and Stock Publishers
199 W. 8th Ave., Suite 3
Eugene, OR 97401

www.wipfandstock.com

PAPERBACK ISBN: 978-1-6667-5981-5
HARDCOVER ISBN: 978-1-6667-5982-2
EBOOK ISBN: 978-1-6667-5983-9

03/01/23

To my beloved Patreon subscribers.

Contents

Preface

THIS BOOK GREW OUT of my experience of trying to pray the prayer-tradition in which I was raised, that of the Orthodox Church, in the different places and circumstances I have found myself in the thirty-two years that I have been a nun. Throughout the last thirty-two years, I went from prayer-life in a monastic community in a convent, to prayer-life on my own in an apartment in the center of a city, and from prayer-life without a constant Internet connection and a mobile phone, to prayer-life in our twenty-four-seven Internet age. The latter transition, from an offline life to one with a constant Internet connection, has radically changed all of our lives, whether we had a "prayer-life" or not. In my case, these transitions changed me profoundly; they have changed the way I perceive time, the way I pray, and the way I perceive the church and what it means to be church.

A few more words about the twists and turns of my rather unconventional monastic journey, as it unfolded since I entered a convent at age nineteen, and until I began working on an online ministry in the center of Vienna, Austria. In September 1990, I entered the Russian Orthodox "Lesna" Convent in Provémont, France. I lived there for five years, from age nineteen to twenty-four, conducting the choir and also working as the gardener and as the "prosphornitsa" (or baker of the "prosphora" that are the eucharistic breads). At age twenty-four, I was transferred to Munich, Germany, by the Russian Orthodox Archbishop of Berlin and Germany. In Munich I lived for almost twelve years in a small monastic community of only two or (at times) three nuns, in an apartment that was attached to the Archbishop's Munich-cathedral, where we nuns chanted the daily services of the Hours in our apartment, and also attended the vigils and Divine Liturgy at the cathedral. I conducted the small choir of the cathedral at weekday-services, and also organized the diocesan church-singing conferences in Munich and Köln, where I taught church-singing and "Ustav" (the order of church-services) together with others. In the late 1990s and early 2000's, the archbishop sent me to the Convent of the Ascension on the Mount of Olives in Jerusalem, where I lived for two years, conducting the convent-choir, teaching novices catechetical courses, and working in one of the guesthouses.

After I returned to Munich from Jerusalem, the Archbishop sent me and one other sister to study Orthodox theology at the Orthodox Institute of the University of Munich. Here I completed my undergraduate and Master's degrees, and then went on to my doctoral studies at the Oriental Pontifical Institute in Rome, where my doctoral dissertation, which focused on the Byzantine Hierarchal Liturgy, was directed by the famous Jesuit scholar of Byzantine Liturgy, Prof. Fr. Robert Taft, SJ.

Here I would like to say a bit more about Fr. Taft, who was not only my academic mentor, but also a formative influence on my prayer-journey. He was an inspiring example of Jesuit spirituality, combining work (in his case, academic work) with a life of prayer. His early-morning "prayer rule," which rather perplexed me at the time, consisted not of reading the "Morning Prayers" of the Prayer Book, but of reading the First Hour. In the early morning, Fr. Taft read the First Hour in Slavonic from his "Chasoslov" or Horologion, before celebrating the Byzantine Divine Liturgy at the Byzantine chapel of the "Russicum," the college attached to the Oriental Institute. At that time, I was not a big fan of the First Hour, because in my church-tradition, the First Hour is a service chanted at the end of vigils, where it makes little sense. This is why I found Taft's morning "pray rule" perplexing. After Divine Liturgy, Fr. Taft had breakfast and read *The New York Times*, and then went to work in the library until noon. At noon, he attended Sext, the Roman Catholic service of the Sixth Hour, together with the Jesuit-community of the Oriental Institute, after which he ate lunch and took a forty-minute nap. Then he would return to the library and worked there until suppertime. As far as I know, he had no evening "prayer rule." He read detective-novels before going to bed at 9 pm, calling this his "junk reading." So, Fr. Taft's daily schedule involved the two prayer-traditions that were part of his life, the Byzantine one that he had learned as the focus of his academic career, and the Roman one in which he was born and raised; and his daily reading included "secular" sources like the newspaper and detective-novels. For me, Fr. Taft remains an inspiring example of living Tradition "in this world," according to one's own background, character, circumstances, and vocation.

I completed my doctorate in 2008, when I was invited to teach liturgical studies at the University of Vienna in Austria. I moved to Vienna, where there was no monastic community, so I began to live in solitude, outside of a monastic community, which was something new for me. While teaching at the University of Vienna, I began to make YouTube videos about the Lives of the Saints of the church-calendar, on a YouTube channel called "Coffee with Sister Vassa."

This YouTube channel, initially a hobby alongside my academic job, developed into the online ministry and corporation that I manage today full-time, "Coffee with Sister Vassa Inc." I left my position at the University of Vienna in 2016 and began to work independently online. Why? For several reasons. First of all, my academic work, e.g., teaching at university, speaking at academic conferences, and publishing in academic periodicals, reached only a small circle of liturgical scholars and the (mostly Roman Catholic) students that attended my lectures and seminars at the Catholic Theological Faculty of the University of Vienna. I wanted to share what I had been studying, the Byzantine liturgical tradition, not only with scholars and students but with the many laypeople who actually lived this tradition, but never had the opportunity to learn its meaning and history. By 2016, with the help of an assistant, I had figured out how to become financially self-supporting through crowd-funding on patreon.com and by selling Coffee with Sister Vassa merchandise (coffee mugs, calendars, a self-published book) from our website. So, when my contract ended with the University of Vienna in 2016, instead of applying for another academic position, I began to work full-time and independently, online. Working online and independently, without any institutional backing, has proven to be both gratifying and enormously difficult on many levels. I would not recommend it to anyone, although I believe it is my vocation and the strange place to which God has led me, for reasons known only to him. But let me turn to the topic of my Internet activity and its effects on my prayer-life.

Among all the twists and turns of my monastic life, as described above, the most drastic change was the transition from an offline-life to an online-life, with constant Internet connectivity, along with the challenges this brings to my prayer-life. Initially it swept me up before I realized what was happening, and I found myself checking my phone throughout much of my days, and eventually even once or twice at night. I could not escape the Internet altogether, and indeed embraced it as a new element of my vocation. By this time, my daily work and vocation were centered in the online ministry of "Coffee with Sister Vassa," which involves producing various catechetical videos, programs, reflections, and other Orthodox Christian content on various Internet platforms, and also interacting with those who comment or ask questions about it on social media.

So, escape was not an option. But the burdensome chaos of twenty-four-seven Internet time compelled me to seek a better way to manage this chaotic time, in a way that fostered, not destroyed, my vocation. I eventually found this "better way" within my own church-tradition, being as I am a product of a specific church-tradition, the Byzantine Orthodox Christian one. This ancient church tradition has at its disposal a now-broken and mostly neglected practice of "ordering" our hours and days by "hallowing" each day and hour with specific prayers and/or sacred memories. I discovered this tradition anew, in the chaotic context of the Internet Age, and the way in which I am learning to utilize it in this context is what I will be sharing in the following pages.

Now, for the acknowledgments to those who helped me along the journey of conceiving and writing this book. First of all, I am grateful to God for the disorienting experience of being swept away by twenty-four-seven Internet time. Without that experience, I could not have related to the laypeople to whom I minister, and with whom I walk through the church-year in our online-community that is "Coffee with Sister Vassa" with its online platforms.

I am most grateful to my subscribers on patreon.com/sistervassa, where I have posted a five-day-a-week audio-podcast, each weekday, for over three years. I reduced the podcast to one day a week six months ago, so that I could find the time to write this book. In the podcast, called "Morning Coffee," I have talked mainly about the liturgical meanings of each weekday, according to Byzantine liturgical tradition. These "meanings" include the liturgical commemorations of each weekday (from the weekly liturgical cycle of the Oktoechos), along with the saint or saints celebrated in the annual liturgical cycle (from the liturgical Menaion), and a Scripture-reading relevant to the day or season. The purpose of the podcast is to help myself and the podcast-subscribers to stay in touch with the Church's liturgical tradition between weekends, on those days when most people do not go to church. The podcast became especially important to me and my listeners during the lockdowns throughout the COVID pandemic, when many of us could not go to church at all. Our online-community, focused on walking through the church-calendar together, was an important way of fostering our sense of church-belonging at a difficult time. I am grateful for the feedback of the listeners, for the insightful and inspiring comments that they have posted under the podcast throughout the years. These comments, along with the subject-matter of the podcast that is church time and the church calendar, have also inspired and informed the content of this book. I also thank my subscribers for their financial support in the last six months, during which I provided them with only one podcast a week, as mentioned above, so that I could have the time to write this book. I thank you, my beloved subscribers, for staying subscribed throughout this time.

Finally, I want to thank Stephen Keeler for editing the initial manuscript. I am also grateful to several wise friends, who took the time to read the chapters of this book as I was writing them, and offered me their theological insights. For this I thank first and foremost Fr. Prof. John Behr, Lynette and Brandon Hull, Lisa Priebe, and last but not least, Fr. Prof. Cyril Hovorun.

Introduction

THE PROBLEM: TIME WITH NEITHER RHYME NOR REASON

IT HAS BEEN SAID that a major problem of our times is that people increasingly lack "purpose" and "meaning" in their lives. Another problem, to this author's mind, is that the most influential people of our day, the tech geniuses and self-help gurus, seem convinced that "we" are the ones who are to create this purpose or meaning for ourselves, just as we invent new technologies, self-help programs, and guidebooks.

Elon Musk talked about this in October 2020, when he identified "meaning" with the "work" (in the sense of employment in the job market) for which human beings are needed less and less, because of automation or robots. "How do people then have meaning?" Musk asks. "A lot of people, they derive their meaning from their employment. So . . . if you're not needed, what's the meaning? Do you have meaning? . . . How do we ensure that the future is going to be the future that we want?"[1] Three years earlier, another leading entrepreneur, Mark Zuckerberg, addressed a similar question in his Harvard commencement speech of May 2017. He established that in the generation of "our parents" you found purpose in "your job, your church, your community," but that this is no longer the case, as automation and globalization has uprooted us from a

1. DB Business, "Elon Musk Warning," 2:44—3:15.

sense of belonging to any of these. "The challenge for our generation," Zuckerberg concluded, "is to *create a world* where everyone has a sense of purpose."[2]

Renowned clinical psychologist and YouTube personality Jordan Peterson, in his international bestseller, *12 Rules for Life: An Antidote to Chaos*, provides answers to the questions posed by the tech geniuses. Peterson argues that we already have "sufficient meaning," within our human psyche. "It is possible," writes Peterson, "to find sufficient meaning in individual consciousness and experience." Differently from the tech geniuses, he looks to psychology, neuroscience, Bible stories, mythology, philosophy, and literature to map out the "12 rules for life" by which we might escape the chaos of meaningless existence. But similar to the tech geniuses, Jordan Peterson seems to see "us" or our human psyche as creators of "meaning"; it is not received from a Creator, as a vocation or call from Another. "We must each tell the truth," Peterson insists, "and repair what is in disrepair and break down and recreate what is old and outdated. It is in this manner that we can and must reduce the suffering that poisons the world."[3] I'll note that I have great respect for Jordan Peterson's earnestness and brilliance as a clinical psychologist, and for many of his insights on Bible stories. But his vision of our human purpose and meaning, also as he finds it in the Bible, sees all of it as a creation of ours or of past generations. According to this vision, God himself is a useful, perhaps even vital, creation of the human psyche, thought up by human beings in the course of their biological evolution to reduce the suffering it involved. And now, as far as I understand Jordan Peterson's message, we must "recreate" him, to maintain our sanity. This vision is fundamentally sad and burdensome, not only because it places the impossible burden of being God on our human shoulders, but because it is untrue. What we are actually invited to receive, as handed down to us in the Bible and in other parts of Christian tradition, is faith; it is faith—first and foremost—in the simple and joyous truth that God *is*. And by "simple and joyous truth" I do not mean that

2. ABC News, "Zuckerberg Harvard Commencement Speech," 7:55—8:02; 8:40–48. Italics mine.

3. Peterson, *12 Rules*, xxxiii.

its reception is easy or effortless. It does take work, quite dignifying daily and hourly work, to nourish our faith in God, and the Bible provides us with this nourishment, along with other parts of Christian tradition. Bible "stories" (both of the Old and New Testaments) may provide us with wise messages and a moral compass, helping us get through the day in synergy and communion with God, but their purpose is not to provide us with a system of lifehacks that will necessarily lead us to "success" and "happiness," in the sense that many self-help programs and gurus aim to do. Their purpose is to foster our faith in the Triune God, by reminding us of his "work" in our world throughout salvation history, and by encouraging us thereby to participate in that creative "work," not on our own but in synergy with him and with all the "communion of the saints" or all those in communion with him. This kind of creative "work," as far as I've experienced it, is joyous, not because it leads me to "success" and "happiness" as I see or imagine those embodied in the celebrities of our world, but because it is done within this great communion, and not on my own.

So, I don't disagree with the leading minds and "builders" of our day, like Elon Musk, Mark Zuckerburg, and Jordan Peterson, that we as human beings need to build, and even to create, in our world. I disagree with them, insofar as they seem to think we can do this building and creating without God, or without participating in God's creative energies. And I vehemently disagree with them, when they suggest that our sense of purpose and belonging can be created or built by us, and us alone. They are thinking along the lines of the builders of the Tower of Babel, who presumed that their building project could secure the unity of human beings, defending them from the dangers of living separately. "Otherwise," they reasoned, "we shall be scattered abroad upon the face of the whole earth" (Gen 11:4b NKJV).

In our Internet age, also known as the Information Age, we are being more "scattered" than unified through the technologies we have built, which can be "dis-orienting." It is not, however, because we no longer have our "Orient" or "orient-ation," which literally means to be "facing *East*" or "the Orient from on high," Who is Christ, our purpose and meaning (our *logos*). It is because we are

3

distracted from him, as were previous generations, but also differently from previous generations, by the many meanings with which we are bombarded twenty-four-seven on the Internet, *with neither rhyme nor reason*. That is to say, the meaning of all this information, received chaotically, does not fit into our lives either poetically or logically. There is no harmony in the chaotic "music" of the disparate news and thoughts shared in the posts through which we may scroll on any given day or at any given hour, and there is no logical order to the times and places where we receive notifications of these. When Shakespeare made the phrase "neither rhyme nor reason" popular in the English language, using it in his play *The Comedy of Errors*, written in 1590, he used it in a question that could be posed about each of us today: "Was there ever any man thus beaten out of season, when in the why and the wherefore is neither rhyme nor reason?"

TIME WITH PRESENCE AND MEANING

Also, our physical and temporal distance from those communicating with us through our computer or phone, not in "real time," may leave us desiring more "presence," both to other human beings and to the natural world in our immediate surroundings. As Hans Ulrich Gumbrecht noted in his discussion of "presence culture" vs. "meaning culture,"[4] knowledge is not only passed on to us secondhand, through its *interpretation*, but also through its immediate *revelation*, in the aesthetics of any given reality, e.g., a work of art. So according to Gumbrecht, our physical presence to, and perception of, the world should go hand-in-hand with learning the meaning of it all.

While Gumbrecht is a literary critic, not dealing with theology or liturgy, his observations are relevant to the topic of this book. That topic is an ancient Christian tradition of walking through our hours and days in a prayerful way, a way that is both a "presence culture" and a "meaning culture." It is the way of the ancient Christian prayer-traditions in both East and West, but in this volume

4. Gumbrecht, *Production of Presence*.

4

we will be focusing on the Eastern Orthodox Christian, Byzantine liturgical tradition, with its feasting-and-fasting rhythm of meaning-filled hours, days, weeks, and seasons. Observing or "keeping watch" over these hours, days, weeks, and seasons, along with their faith-based purpose, enables us to be present to each moment. It helps us not to be carried unawares through time, which in and of itself is chaotic and even "evil," as Saint Paul observes, "for the days are evil" (Eph 5:16 NKJV). This "evil" time is the not-ordered kind, or un-disciplined time, which requires the redemptive and creative ordering of it by God's word, which is carried and shared in this world by "redeemers of the time" (*exagorazomenoi ton kairon*, Eph 5:16), all Christians.

REDEEMING THE TIME

What does it mean, to "redeem" the time? To "redeem" (from the Latin "re," *back*, and "emere," *to buy*), literally means *to buy back*; as in the Greek word used by Saint Paul, *ex-agorazo*, which means *to buy out*. It means to pay a certain price for something/someone previously ours, but now either imprisoned or owned by someone else. Time, when we do not take ownership of it by ordering it in light of God's word, is a chaotic mess that will carry us through its changes and transitions unawares. So, we need to *buy it back*, paying the price, so to say, of offering ourselves onto the cross, and walking the cross-carrying journey. The whole business of "redeeming the time" is already done by the Son of God, by his stepping into it in his incarnation, and "accepting" it throughout his own cross-carrying life, which he proclaims to be "the acceptable year of the Lord" (Luke 4:19; Isa 61:2 NKJV). Just as he accepted it, so are we called to accept it, in the cross-carrying way as did he. Note also that already in the Old Testament, God recognized the *changeability* of our time, with its constant transitions from night to day, from one season to the next, etc., as a "good" thing; first, when he created the planets on the fourth day (Gen 1:18), and when he promised Noah after the flood: "While the earth remains, seedtime and harvest, cold and heat, winter and summer, and day and night shall not cease" (Gen 8:22 NKJV).

All Christians are dignified with the call to this human-divine "work," to "redeem the time" we are given, by ordering it in the light of God's word. It is through this constant "work," on an hourly and daily basis, that we nourish and keep alive our faith in Christ, and it is through that living faith that we remain in communion with him and the entire "communion of the saints." This communion or "marriage," of Christ and his church (Eph 5:32), requires work, just like any marriage and relationship takes work, so that faith or trust is maintained. This is why our Lord identified faith as "*the* work of God," when the people asked him, "*What shall we do, that we may work the works of God?*" And he responded, "*This is the work of God, that you believe in Him whom He sent*" (John 6:28–29 NKJV).

FOSTERING UNITY AND BELONGING IN TIME

Here's another aspect of the Liturgy of Time, which fosters our human sense of belonging. The liturgical times are "celebrated" (from the Latin *celebrare*, meaning "to assemble to honor"), so that the honoring of these times serves to "assemble" or gather those honoring them. Because this "assembly" involves also those beyond the time-zones and geographical borders of this world, within the Communion of the Saints, it also extends beyond our time zones, borders, and politics. Thus, it effects unity and a sense of belonging among all "celebrants," within the timeless and spaceless presence of God. All are united in the one "Now" (*nyn* in Greek and *nyne* in Slavonic) and the one "Today" (*simeron* in Greek, and *dnes'* in Slavonic) of any given liturgical service or feast, whenever it is remembered in prayer, anywhere around the globe.

So, we need not wonder, together with Elon Musk and Mark Zuckerberg, what kind of "work" can give us a sense of purpose and belonging, in these postmodern times. We have it cut out for us, even if/when we might find ourselves unemployed in the job-market, and if/when we are dispersed throughout a globalized world.

FOSTERING CREATION IN AND
WITH THE CREATOR, IN TIME

The Liturgy of Time, as maintained in the ancient Byzantine liturgical rite, invites one to foster, nay, participate in, God's creative work. How?

First of all, we lend our "It is good" to God's initial "It is good" (Gen 1), by regularly and gratefully "remembering" his seven-day creative work on each day of our seven-day week. We also praise God for creation in the daily evening-service of Vespers and in the morning-services of Matins and the First Hour (or Prime, as it is called in Western Christian traditions), which celebrate God as the Creator of light.

The liturgical services and themes of each day and hour, as we "remember" them in prayer, also draw us into reading or discerning the "signs and seasons," as well as the "days and years," which God provided on the fourth day of creation, when he gave form to time. As described in Gen 1:14–19, on the fourth day God created the sun, moon, stars, and planets "for signs and seasons, and for days and years." This was part of the Creator's ordering of the universe, although there were as yet no other living beings, none of us, to *read* the "signs and seasons" and "days and years" created by him at this point. We were to be on the receiving-end of the God-given "signs" of time, which we are continuously called to read and celebrate as manifestations of his glory, and to his greater glory.

As we profess our "It is good" to God's creation on a daily basis, along with reading the "signs" of God-given time(s) not just individually or haphazardly but according to church-tradition, we do so as the unified and unifying "church." Please note this point, because it is important and particularly dignifying. As "church" or "ecclesia" (from the Greek verb *ek-kaleo*, meaning *to call forth* or *to call out*), which is the sacrament of unity, of the unity of all those "called" by God, we foster the unity of all creation by responding to his "call" in time and in step with a common prayer-tradition.

Our participation in the prayer tradition of the hours and days is also profoundly *creative*, drawing us into participation in God's creative work in our own ways, in the context of our own time.

7

Metropolitan Kallistos Ware writes about this creative aspect of reliving tradition as follows: "Our reliving of Tradition is essentially creative. . . . To be a true traditionalist is to be creative. What is tradition? It is creative life. And what is creativity? It is the reinterpretation of tradition in the context of our present-day experience."[5]

A VOCATION OF BOTH MONASTICS AND LAYPEOPLE

One might ask, doesn't all this only work in a monastery, where a full cycle of church services is celebrated on a daily basis? No, it can and does work also outside the context of a monastery and even outside church services, as will be described in the following pages. More will be said about the ecclesiological implications of the Liturgy of Time, or what is means for our church-being, in the final chapter of this book.

THE PURPOSE AND SCOPE OF THIS BOOK

This book will focus on: 1. The daily "Little" Hours (the First, Third, Sixth, and Ninth Hours), with a brief addendum on the "Big" Hour of Vespers, found in the Byzantine Horologion or *Chasoslov* in Slavonic; and 2. The liturgical commemorations of the days of the week, governed by the Oktoechos or "Oktoich." It will not focus on the annual liturgical cycles of the feasts and fasting-seasons, i.e., Christmas, Lent and Pascha/Easter, Pentecost, nor on the saints of every calendar day, because each of these liturgical cycles require a book of their own. The final chapter of the book will discuss the ecclesiological implications of the Liturgy of Time, or what it means for our church-being, our being as church, within time.

The primary purpose of this book is not theoretical or academic, but practical; it is to provide just enough theological and historical information about the liturgical hours and days to incentivize the reader to begin praying these, simply and practically, on a daily basis. One will not find in the following pages a description

5. Ware, "Tradition and Creativity," 21.

of the historical development of the Daily Office in the Byzantine Rite, nor of the Oktoechos liturgical system of weekdays. Providing the modern-day reader with an understanding of the meaning(s) of each weekday and each daily "Hour," as these are handed down to us in our day in the Byzantine liturgical tradition, along with practical prayer tips, this book aims to encourage the reader to live and pray these hours and weekdays in the context of our twenty-four-seven Internet age. If you, my reader, put any or all of what is suggested in this book into practice, the primary purpose of this book will have been accomplished.

A second purpose of this book is to provide an alternative point of entry into the resolution of an ecclesiological problem we find ourselves in today, particularly (but not only) in the Orthodox churches. It is the problem of neglecting the historical aspect of the church's being, or of *the church's being within time.* This leads us in the Orthodox churches to a distorted or ahistorical vision of church-tradition, as something that supposedly "never changed" and must never be changed. It also leads us to various reductionist ecclesi-ologies, which see "the church" not as embodied in every member thereof at every time and every day, but as something manifested almost exclusively in the doings and sayings of its hierarchy/clergy, and in the Eucharist that cannot be celebrated without them. We tend to identify "the church" with its hierarchy when we focus our church-being on the church-political activities and disputes of our patriarchs, the Pope, and other hierarchs among themselves; when we focus on the personalities and shortcomings or strengths of our parish-priests; and when we either join or leave the church because of these. We also identify "the church" primarily with its hierarchy/clergy when we limit our church-belonging to going on Sundays and major feasts to the Eucharist, that is, to Mass or Divine Liturgy, which is presided over by our clergy, with more or less participation of the laity. By doing so, we profess a kind of "Eucharistic eccle-siology" (whether or not we are aware of it), which some of the best and brightest Orthodox and Roman Catholic theologians of the twentieth century reflected on, including the Orthodox theolo-gians Nikolai Afanasiev (+1966), George Florovsky (+1979), Paul Evdokimov (+1970), and John Zizioulas (+2023), and the Roman

Catholic Cardinal Henri de Lubac (+1991), Yves Congar (+1995), Louis Bouyer (+2004), Emmanuel Lanne (+2010), and Joseph Cardinal Ratzinger/Pope Benedict XVI (+2022). It would exceed the scope and purpose of this little book to analyze the "Eucharistic ecclesiology" of these theologians, but suffice it to say here, in fairness to them, that they more or less balance this ecclesiology by emphasizing the importance of other aspects of church-life outside the Eucharist. Here I am focusing on an "ecclesiological problem" not as it is expressed in academic theology, but as it plays out in our (not unrelated) church practice, in which we tend to be in church and to "be church" only at the Eucharist, while our Liturgy of the Hours remains broken and neglected. This is a "problem," I would suggest, because it obfuscates and diminishes the role of all of us, both clergy and laity, as church, outside the eucharistic context. It also obfuscates and diminishes the meaning of time itself, as we walk through it on our cross-carrying journeys, hour by hour and day after day. In the following pages, dedicated to praying the liturgical Hours and weekdays, I would like to help us learn to see ourselves as church, also outside the eucharistic context and at every moment.

1

The Hours

HISTORICAL BACKGROUND

THE "WORK" THAT IS "redeeming the time" and nourishing our faith is not just a Sunday thing, nor is it a special monastic privilege. It is an hourly and daily vocation of all Christians. The dignifying challenge of "ordering" our time in the light of faith, then, confronts all of us, everywhere, and at every hour. The various ancient traditions of praying at certain times of the day, for example, the Jewish custom observed by the apostles sometimes in the temple (Acts 3:1), of praying three times a day at the third, sixth, and ninth "hours" (according to the sundial), or the somewhat later custom of seven fixed prayer times mentioned in other ancient Christian sources, were often done privately (cf. Acts 10:9) and, before the rise of organized monasticism in the fourth century, by laypeople. For example, the late-first-century church order, the *Didache*, instructs all members of its community to pray the Our Father thrice daily (*Did.* 8:11). The daily prayer-times were not celebrated together by the entire church-community, when gathering as a community several times a day was impractical and in times of persecution dangerous.

The transition from the sundial to the mechanical clock proved both a blessing and a curse, so to say, for our Christian vocation of "redeeming the time." Just as the introduction of virtual, twenty-four-seven time in our Internet age provides both blessings and an overload of things to keep up with, so did the mechanical clock increase the demands on our time and productivity, which affected our traditioned prayer-times. As Nicholas Carr observes in his important book, *The Shallows: What the Internet Is Doing to Our Brains*:

> For most of human history, people experienced time as a continuous, cyclical flow. To the extent that time was "kept," the keeping was done by instruments that emphasized this natural process: sundials around which shadows would move, hourglasses down which sand would pour, clepsydras through which water would stream. There was no particular need to measure time with precision or to break a day up in little pieces. For most people, the movements of the sun, the moon, and the stars provided the only clocks they needed. Life was, in the words of the French medievalist Jacques Le Goff, "dominated by agrarian rhythms, free of haste, careless of exactitude, unconcerned by productivity.[1]

It was in the late Middle Ages, and specifically by Western Christian monks, as Carr further describes, that the need for more temporal exactitude was felt and the technologies of timekeeping were pushed forward:

> It was in the monastery that the first mechanical clocks were assembled, their movements governed by the swinging of weights, and it was the bells in the church tower that first sounded the hours by which people would come to parcel out their lives. The desire for accurate timekeeping spread outward from the monastery. . . . As people moved from the countryside to the town and started working in the markets, mills and factories rather than fields, their days came to be carved into ever more finely sliced segments, each announced by the tolling of a bell. . . . The need for tighter scheduling and synchronization

---

1. Carr, *Shallows*, 44.

of work, transport, devotion, and even leisure provided
the impetus for rapid progress in clock technology.[2]

I think that the Liturgy of the Hours, while it inspired the
introduction of the mechanical "clock" (from the medieval Latin
word "clocca," *bell*), never recovered from this technological stride.
At the latest by the fourteenth century, when the mechanical clock
had become commonplace in Europe, the Liturgy of the Hours
began to be "too much," and to spiral into the disarray in which
it is today, both in East and West. The increased demands on our
time and productivity, both in parishes and monasteries, in the best
cases pushes the Hours from their proper times to the beginnings
and ends of the workday, and in the worst cases leads to liturgical
absurdities, such as celebrating Matins in the evening and Vespers
in the morning in Byzantine Rite churches. It is for this reason that
Fr. Taft admitted in the introduction to his book, *The Liturgy of the
Hours in East and West*, that writing about the Daily Office in our
day feels like "giving a transfusion to a cadaver."[3]

Yet the Orthodox Church seems never to have noticed the
"problem" of the radical change that took place in our liturgical tradition as a result of the transition from the sundial to the mechanical clock. And there was never any opposition to this transition,
as there was in the early twentieth century, to the far less consequential transition of some Orthodox churches from the Julian
Calendar to the Gregorian. It appears we are willing to accept even
radical changes to our timekeeping tradition, as long as "we" do not
take responsibility for them. This way, we can uphold the myth that
"our" tradition never changed, because "we" never changed it—as if
this were a good thing! However, the undeniable fact of the changeability both of calendars and other timekeeping technologies, along
with their effects on church life, should alert us to the vital necessity
for more reflection on the blind spot in Orthodox ecclesiology that
is the theology of time.

In this book we will not be reviewing other aspects of the well-
researched history of the Liturgy of the Hours, because our purpose

2. Carr, *Shallows*, 42.

3. Taft, *Liturgy of the Hours*, xii.

is to focus on re-discovering it in our day, in very practical terms. We will discuss the prayer tradition of the daytime "Little" Hours of the Byzantine Rite, along with the "Big" Hour of Vespers, exploring both why and how we might pray these Hours in a simplified way and privately, even amidst a busy work schedule.

THE "LITTLE HOURS" IN CHURCH-PRACTICE TODAY

What are the "Little" or "Minor" Hours? They are distinguished from the "Big" or "Major" Hours of the daily church-services, known as "Vespers" (the big evening service) and "Matins" (the big morning service). The Little Hours of the liturgical day, usually less familiar to laypeople, are known as the First Hour (Prime), Third Hour (Terce), Sixth Hour (Sext), and Ninth Hour (None). They correspond to the times of day as rendered by a sundial, as will be explained below, and are meant to be prayed at these times, throughout the (work)day.

Because these Hours are meant to be prayed throughout the (work)day, when it is impractical to gather for communal prayer, they do not really "work" on the communal level, either in monasteries or parishes. In practice they are either omitted altogether, or celebrated in a row, one after the other, attached to the beginning or end of one of the "Big" Hours, or of the Divine Liturgy, for which the community does gather. But even when people do happen to be in church for the Little Hours, say, for the Third and Sixth Hours before Divine Liturgy, these twenty-or-so minutes are usually dedicated to some activity *other than* praying these Hours, like venerating the icons, buying and lighting candles, going to confession, having a quick choir rehearsal, etc. Even the parish priest is occupied with something else, during the Hours, like completing the Proskomide or hearing confessions.

Thus, the whole point of the Hours, which is to help us "redeem the time" of day for which each Hour is meant, and to re-present us in prayer to God *at their specific times* and through the meaning attached to each of these times, is lost. This corrosion of the hourly prayer tradition is evident also in the case of the "Big" Hours, as can be observed in the widespread custom of celebrating Matins in the evening, and Vespers in the morning. It is not surprising that the whole point and value also of the "Big" Hours of Vespers and Matins appears to be lost on most of the faithful, as the poor church attendance of these services in almost any parish would suggest. The faithful do not find time for these services, I think, not because we do not have time, but because we do not quite understand their point and hence do not treasure them. To put it a different way, our "hearts" are not in these services, because we do not regard these services as our "treasures." "For where your treasure is," after all, "there will your heart be also" (Matt 6:21 NKJV).

THE PRAYER BOOK REPLACES
THE TRADITIONAL HOURS

Many faithful do pray in the mornings and evenings, by some version of the "Prayer Book," called *Molitvoslov* in Slavonic and *Prosevchitarion* in Greek. The Slavonic *Molitvoslov* originates in the seventeenth century (and the Greek *Prosevchitarion* even later), and contains Morning and Evening Prayers, along with Prayers of Preparation for Holy Communion, Prayers After Holy Communion, Akathist hymns and other popular devotions. These prayers, mostly focusing our attention on our individual sins and repentance, were originally meant as an optional complement to the traditional liturgical services. In practice, however, they have become surrogates for the latter. As the traditional liturgical services have increasingly become incomprehensible for most people, the more-comprehensible private devotions of the Prayer Book have come to fill a vacuum. In some churches, such as the Russian Orthodox Church, the lengthy Morning and Evening Prayers, and Prayers before and after Communion, are even considered mandatory for all the faithful.

There is nothing wrong with complementing the liturgical services with additional private prayers, if one has the inclination to do so. However, there is a problem with replacing the traditional Daily

Office with them, and/or making these surrogates mandatory as an additional burden on the shoulders of the faithful. For example, it is unreasonable, in Russian Orthodox parishes, to expect the faithful to come home in the late evening after an "All Night Vigil," (a service that contains Vespers, Matins and the First Hour and that lasts about two or three hours), and then to read the Evening Prayers that in my *Molitvoslov* or Prayer Book are twenty-three pages long. The following morning, before going to church for the Third and Sixth Hours and Divine Liturgy, the faithful are expected to read the Morning Prayers of the Prayer Book at home. Also, if one intends to approach Holy Communion at Divine Liturgy, one is also obliged to read at some point (before or after the Vigil, or in the morning before Liturgy) the lengthy Rule Before Holy Communion. These private devotions of the Prayer Book are deemed necessary, I think, because the liturgical services themselves, i.e., Vespers, Matins, the Little Hours and even Divine Liturgy itself have become largely incomprehensible.

I think that the relatively new practice of replacing the Hours with private prayers is not a good thing, and not because it is a relatively new thing. Our prayer tradition has undergone many changes, edifying changes and innovations that helped us as church to profess in daily prayer our theology and ecclesiological vision, as it was articulated and refined by the Councils and saints throughout the centuries. But the change from the Hours to prayers of the Prayer Book was neither edifying or helpful, theologically or ecclesiologically. This is not because the Hours are more ancient than the prayers of the Prayer Book, but because the Hours do for us what the prayers do not. The Hours draw us into the biblical and theological mind of the church, helping us adopt and embrace that mind at every hour of every day, as we will see below.

REDISCOVERING THE HOURS
AS A LAYPERSON TODAY

I suggest we could dust off the forgotten treasure of tradition that is the Liturgy of the Hours, rediscover its value, and put it to work for us in our common Christian enterprise of "redeeming the time." We might do so with the gentle realism that is humility, which respects the possibilities and limitations of living tradition within our own historical context. Rather than adopting an everything-or-nothing attitude regarding the traditioned Little Hours, we could re-discover the power of praying them, by doing so in a simplified manner. This "simplified manner," described at length in this chapter, includes:

1. Focusing on the main "theme" of each Little Hour, as expressed in its main hymn or *Troparion*, at its proper time of day. The Troparion of the Hour is nowadays only chanted during the weekday-services of Lent, while on all other days of the year it came to be replaced by the Troparion of the saint/feast of the day. Nonetheless, there is nothing specifically "Lenten" about the Troparion of the Hour; it is retained within the liturgical "high season" of Lent, because the "high seasons" of the liturgical year retain the most ancient forms of liturgical rites. The Troparion of the Hour belongs to the most ancient stratum of the Byzantine Little Hours. It is found in our oldest manuscript of the Byzantine monastic office, the ninth-century Horologion *Sinai gr. 863*, in which it is chanted every day.[4] While it may be unfamiliar to most faithful, I suggest it is worth the trouble, of memorizing each of the Troparia of the Hours, because they express the main "theme" of each Hour.
2. Adding to it several Psalm-verses or other brief prayers appropriate to each Hour.

THE TIMES AND THEMES OF
THE LITTLE HOURS

Before we get to the "Troparion," Psalms, and other details of each Little Hour, here is a summary of their times and themes. As mentioned earlier, the traditional Hours of daily prayer are based not on the mechanical clock, but on the sundial, according to which each

4. Alexopoulos, "Minor Hours," 235.

"hour" lasts for approximately three of our mechanical clock hours. Here are the timespans, according to the mechanical clock, which correspond to the daytime "hours" of the sundial:

- First Hour—from sunrise to about 9 am

- Third Hour—from about 9 am to about 12 noon

- Sixth Hour—from about 12 noon to about 3 pm

- Ninth Hour—from about 3 pm to about 6 pm

The approximate, not exact, time of these Hours of prayer simplifies matters for busy laypeople: We have about a three-hour window, within which one might remember the *theme* of each of these prayer-times, and focus on it at least briefly, in a simple prayer. Note that the timespan of the First Hour, according to the mechanical clock, changes throughout the year, because it begins at sunrise, which happens at different times throughout the year.

What is meant by the "theme" of each Hour? Each Hour has a certain, special topic or commemoration, as expressed in its psalms and central hymn or Troparion. The theme of each Hour serves as a motivation for prayer; it gives us a reason to pray, specific to each Hour, and as such is an aid to prayer, or to maintaining our communion with God. Here are the themes of the daytime Hours:

- First Hour—Morning, Light

- Third Hour—Pentecost, Descent of the Holy Spirit

- Sixth Hour—The Crucifixion (the nailing of Christ to the Cross)

- Ninth Hour—The Death of Christ on the Cross

Let us next look more closely at each of the daytime Hours, to see how we can pray them amidst any schedule.

THE FIRST HOUR

The First Hour prayer service, known as "Prime" in Western traditions,[5] is meant to be celebrated at some point between sunrise

5. Prime was suppressed in the Roman Catholic tradition by The Second

and about 9 am. Its main theme, or the motivation it offers us for prayer at this time of day, is the time of day itself, early morning or sunrise. It is when we wake up from sleep, and re-establish our conscious connection with time, usually with a glance at our alarm clock. When we wake up in the morning, we also want to re-establish our conscious connection with God. The First Hour prayer service is meant to accompany us through this transition from sleep and darkness (or unawareness of God and time) to watchfulness and awareness of God's light and presence within our time. Hence its main Troparion hymn and Psalms (5, 89/90, and 100/101)[6] focus on connecting a *historical moment*, our morning/sunrise, with the *meaning* it has for us, as the time to make a re-connection with God, recognizing him as the primary source of light and life.

Pss 5, 89/90, and 100/101, of the First Hour

The first of the three Psalms of the First Hour, *Ps 5* ("Give ear to my words, O Lord"), is selected for the First Hour prayer-service because it thematizes morning prayer: "In the morning You shall hear my voice. In the morning shall I stand before You, and You shall look upon me" (Ps 5:2). A large part of Ps 5 also expresses an abhorrence for the ways of evil-doers, on the one hand, and a love for God's righteousness, on the other (Ps 5:3–13), so that from our very waking moment we profess our conscious choice of good over evil. More specifically, we choose to be with God and to orient our steps and gaze toward His "house," lest we begin our day disoriented: "But as for me, in the multitude of Your mercy shall I go into Your house; I shall worship toward Your holy temple" (Ps 5:6).

Vatican Council and was also dropped in The Church of England's Book of Common Prayer. While it remains in the Horologion of the Byzantine Rite, it is often either omitted or abbreviated in Orthodox and Greek Catholic Churches, and/or chanted immediately after Matins. Because Matins is often celebrated in the evening (in Russian Orthodox and related traditions), this means that the First Hour, if chanted at all, is chanted in the evening, where it makes no sense.

6. Most of the Psalms are numbered slightly differently in the Hebrew and Greek (Septuagint) Bibles. Both numbers are indicated in this book, when they are different in the Hebrew and Greek Bibles.

The second of the three Psalms of the First Hour, *Pss 89/90* ("Lord, You have been our refuge in generation and generation"), is selected for the First Hour of our day because it helps us to approach time itself in a faith-enlightened manner. Psalm 89/90 relativizes our time, by stressing that God always "is," before any time or other creation began: "Before the mountains came to be and the earth was formed and the world, even from everlasting to everlasting, You are" (Pss 89/90:2). We are reminded that our years, our lifespans, are but fleeting moments in the light of God's eternal being: "For a thousand years in Your eyes, O Lord, are but as yesterday that is past, and as a watch in the night. Things of no account shall their years be; in the morning like grass shall man pass away" (Pss 89/90:4–5). The point of the Psalm is not to discourage us by depreciating our limited time, as if it were of little import what "work" we do or do not do within it. The point is to help us wake up to it in our morning with a sense of urgency, precisely because we have very little of it. And it is to encourage us to "fill" our time, already in the morning, with God's eternal mercy and brightness: "We were filled in the morning with Your mercy, O Lord, and we rejoiced and were glad... And let the brightness of the Lord our God be upon us, and the works of our hands do guide aright upon us, yea, the work of our hands do guide aright" (Pss 89/90:16, 19). Psalm 89/90 thus invites us to re-affirm the value of both our time and our "work," in God's light, lest we fall into despondency, as if it didn't matter. As we wake up and open our eyes to see natural light (of the rising sun), and/or turn the lights on, Pss 89/90 also teaches us to perceive these lights in our physical world as reminders of God's "brightness." The final Prayer of the First Hour, "O Christ, the true Light," refers this light-theme to Christ, as One Who "enlightens every man who comes into the world."[7]

The third of the three Psalms of the First Hour, *Pss 100/101* ("I will sing of mercy and judgment unto You, O Lord"), consists mainly of affirming our dedication to the "blameless path" in our

7. An almost-identical Prayer of the First Hour is already found in the oldest manuscript of the Byzantine Monastic Office, the ninth-century Horologion, *Sinai gr. 863* (Mateos, "Un Horologion inédit," 51–54. Cf. Alexopoulos, "Minor Hours," 236–37).

"house" that is "the city of the Lord," on the one hand, and affirming our uncompromising hatred for all evil-doing, on the other. This Psalm is chanted at the First Hour because it mentions the "morning" in its final verse: "In the morning I slew all the sinners of the land, utterly to destroy out of the city of the Lord all them that work iniquity" (Pss 100/101:9). Note that we understand "sinners" and "all them that work iniquity" to mean the invisible evil spirits and, importantly, the weaker sides of our own selves, with their potential for befriending these evil spirits.

How Can We Pray the First Hour?

In modern-day Orthodox and Greek Catholic parishes, the First Hour is either omitted altogether (in Greek Orthodox practice), or it is prayed immediately after Matins (in Russian, Ukrainian, and related traditions). Because Matins is usually celebrated in the evening in Slavic practice, apart from Lenten weekdays, the First Hour is usually chanted in the evening, where it makes no sense. It is understandable, then, that most faithful pay little attention to the First Hour, which in parish-churches is chanted at the very end of Vigil. By the end of Vigil, most parishioners have either already gone home, and the few that have remained even up to the First Hour use this moment to venerate the icons, to go to confession, or to do something *else*—something that makes more sense to them than the First Hour, being chanted in the latter hours of the evening.

How can we begin to re-discover the First Hour? We can pray this Hour every day, simply by chanting aloud, or saying to ourselves, its main Troparion hymn, at any point from the moment we wake up to about 9 am. We can also insert in between the Troparion, if we keep repeating it throughout this three-hour window, certain verses from the Psalms of the First Hour, or other brief prayers as suggested below. The Troparion is a paraphrase of several verses from the first of the three Psalms of the First Hour, Ps 5:

First-Hour Troparion:

"In the morning hear my voice, / my King and my God." (Ps 5:2a, 1b)

In between repetitions of the Troparion, we can insert other verses from Psalms of the First Hour, e.g.:

Verses to Insert Between Repetitions of the First-Hour Troparion:

- *"Give ear to my words, O Lord; hear my cry."* (Ps 5:1a)
- *"For unto You will I pray, O Lord."* (Ps 5:1b)
- *"And let the brightness of the Lord our God be upon us, and the works of our hands do guide aright upon us, yea, the work of our hands do guide aright."* (Pss 89/90:19)

If we don't happen to know these verses by heart, we could alternatively insert some other prayer that we do know, e.g.:

Other Prayers to Insert Between Repetitions of the First-Hour Troparion:

- (Jesus Prayer) *"Lord, Jesus Christ, Son of God, have mercy on me, the sinner."*
- (The Lord's Prayer) *"Our Father . . ."*
- (To the Theotokos) *"Most Holy Theotokos, save us!"*
- (To the Saint of the Day) *"Holy (Martyr, Father, Mother, etc.) N, pray to God for us!"*
- (On Mondays) *"Holy Archangels and Angels, pray to God for us!"*[8]
- (On Sundays) *"Glory be, O Lord, to Your holy resurrection!"*
- (On Saturdays) *"All Saints, pray to God for us!"*

---

8. For more on the weekday-commemorations, see chapter 2.

Additional Practical Tips

1. *The Sequence of Troparion and Verses*: To be clear, in case any readers out there do not understand what it means to "insert" certain verses or prayers "between repetitions of the Troparion," what it means is this: We first say the First-Hour Troparion (aloud or to ourselves), "In the morning hear my voice, my King and my God." Then we say the verse, "Give ear to my words, O Lord: hear my cry." After this verse, we again say the First-Hour Troparion, "In the morning hear my voice, my King and my God." Then we say the other verse, "For unto You will I pray, O Lord." And then, again, we pray the First-Hour Troparion, "In the morning hear my voice, my King and my God." And we follow that either with the same verses, or we can use other verses or prayers listed above, e.g., those appropriate to the weekday. For example, on Mondays we can say, after one of our repetitions of the First-Hour Troparion, "Holy Archangels and Angels, pray to God for us!"

2. *Memorize the Troparion and Verses*: It is important to learn by heart at least the Troparion, which (in the case of the First-Hour Troparion) is very brief, so this will be easy. We might write it down on a post-it, along with the two main verses of the Hour, while we are new to practicing this prayer discipline, and we can stick this Post-it onto our bedside table or onto the mirror above our bathroom sink, wherever we will see it in the morning. We can use this method also for the rest of the Hours, writing down their Troparia and verses on Post-its, while we are learning them by heart.

3. *Do Not Give Up*: But we shouldn't be discouraged or give up on praying the Hours, while we don't know these texts by heart, or when we repeatedly lose focus and tend to forget about them. It is a lifelong process, learning to pray; some days and hours will always be less focused than others, but as we keep returning to our simple prayer discipline, our little, inner prayer clock continues to develop. Our little bit of prayer discipline is like a mustard seed that grows slowly but surely

into a sturdy tree, large enough to provide us (and others in our midst) with the "shade" of God's grace in the heat of difficult moments.

4. *Keep Things Simple*: It is important to keep this prayer simple, so that it is doable and sustainable within a busy schedule. Don't overthink or overcomplicate the way that to you it.

5. *Keep the Phone and Computer Turned Off*: It is a good idea *not* to turn on our phone or computer, before praying the First Hour in this simple way, so that our focus in the early morning is not immediately distracted or scattered from God to everyone and everything else.

6. *Praying Amidst Inevitable Distractions or Disruptions*: Even if our early morning involves inevitable distractions, for example, if we have small children or others for whom we must care at home, as we go about our morning routine, preparing breakfast for the family, etc., we can pray this brief Troparion to ourselves, "*In the morning hear my voice, my King and my God,*" perhaps just once or twice. Or if our morning prayer-schedule is disrupted because we've overslept, we can still fall back on this informal way of praying, and sing or say to ourselves the Troparion in the shower, during our drive to work, and so on, until about 9 am, when the time comes to pray the Third Hour in a similar manner.

7. *Formalize this Prayer, from Time to Time:* It is helpful to formalize our hourly prayer, from time to time, when possible. How? We can stand before our icons, pray the Troparion of the Hour, making the sign of the cross and doing a small prostration. Doing these physical motions helps us re-focus on the meaning of the Troparion of the Hour, when praying it becomes so habitual that we lose sight of its meaning.

The way the First Hour happens in my everyday life, in an apartment in the center of a busy European city, is that I sing this brief Troparion, immediately after waking up at around 4 or 5 am (I usually need to get up early, because I have to post online a morning audio podcast and daily reflection on Scripture). And I keep repeating it, with different verses inserted in between. I prefer to use the verses from Psalm 5 and the one from Pss 89/90, "And let the brightness" as I make my bed, wash my face, make my coffee, prepare my breakfast (to be eaten later at 7 am), and after I pray my more-formalized prayers and sit down at my computer. My phone, turned off at night, gets turned on later, at 9 am at the earliest.

The Troparion, "*In the morning hear my voice, my King and my God,*" places me before the eyes of God, so to say, and helps me immediately to recognize him as my primary authority, as both "my King" and "my God," even before I do my formalized prayers. This Troparion echoes the resolve each candidate for Holy Baptism expresses immediately before saying the Creed in the rite of Reception into the Catechumenate, which precedes Baptism. After the candidate (or sponsor/godparent) renounces Satan, "breathes and spits" on him toward the West, he or she turns to the East and professes unity and faith in Christ "as King and God," in response to the priest's questions:

> Priest: *Have you united yourself to Christ?*
> Candidate: *I have united myself to Christ.*
> Priest: *Do you believe in Him?*
> Candidate: *I believe in Him as King and God.*[9]

Praying the First-Hour Troparion every morning, calling to God as "my King and my God," is a way to re-affirm the decision professed at Baptism.

I especially love verse 19 of Ps 90, "*And let the brightness of the Lord our God be upon us, and the works of our hands do guide aright upon us, yea, the work of our hands do guide aright,*" because it shines this bright light on my morning's "work," or "the work of my hands" as I make my bed, prepare breakfast, and type away at the computer in the early morning. The light theme of this verse also helps me to be present, in a God-focused way, to the natural phenomenon of the rising sun. The other really neat thing about this way of praying is that I can also fall back on it on days when I am not able to do my formalized morning-prayers, either because I have overslept or for some other reason.

---

9. Orthodox Church in America, "Baptism," 6.

THE THIRD HOUR

The Third Hour prayer service (Terce), is meant to be celebrated at some point between about 9 am and 12 noon. Its main *theme* in its Byzantine version, or the motivation it offers us for prayer at this time of day, is our grateful remembrance of one of the most important events of salvation history that happened at this time of day, *Pentecost*, or the descent of the Holy Spirit on the apostles (cf. Acts 2: 15). The third psalm of the Byzantine Third Hour (Pss 50/51) and its main Troparion hymn reflect this Pentecost theme, which we employ so as to call upon the Holy Spirit to be "renewed" in our hearts in the first part of our (work)day.

There are also two other, lesser-known themes of the Third Hour, namely, *Christ's Trial before Pilate* (cf. Matt 27:1–2) and *Eve's Tasting of the Forbidden Fruit* (and her consequent redemption), both of which are traditionally believed to have taken place at around the Third Hour (about 9 am), and both of which still figure prominently in the Third Hour celebration of several non-Byzantine Eastern Christian traditions. In the Byzantine Third Hour, these two themes are less prominent than the Pentecost theme, but they inspire the first two of the three psalms of this service, Pss 16/17 and 24/25, and lend the service its penitential character.

Pss 16/17, 24/25, and 50/51, of the Third Hour

The first of the three psalms of the Third Hour, *Pss 16/17* ("Hearken, O Lord, unto my righteousness") is placed within this service because it reflects the theme of *Christ's Trial before Pilate*, or his prayer to the Father as he stands before Pilate:

> From before Your face let my judgment come forth. . . .
> You have proved my heart, You have visited it in the night, You have tried me by fire, and unrighteousness was not found in me. . . My enemies have surrounded my soul, they have enclosed themselves with their own fat, their mouth has spoken pride." (Ps 16/17:2a, 3, 9b, 10)

The final verse of the psalm anticipates our Lord's resurrection: "I shall be satisfied when Your glory is made manifest in me" (Pss 16/17:16b). We make this prayer our own, on our own cross-carrying journey, even as we remember his throughout this later part of our morning. And as always, when we speak of our "enemies" in the Psalms, we understand not human beings in our midst, like certain work-colleagues, employees, or a difficult boss. We understand rather those temptations that we might experience through conflicts or other situations or tests of faith that may occur through our interactions with the people, places, and things in our lives, like resentment, jealousy, lust, self-centered fear, idle talk, love of power, despondency, procrastination, etc. We pray that our "righteousness" win over our darker sides, which are our true "enemies," of which we need to be aware and which we hand over to God.

The second of the three psalms of the Third Hour, *Pss 24/25* ("Unto You, O Lord, have I lifted up my soul"), reflects another event remembered at this time of day, *Eve's Tasting of the Forbidden Fruit* (and her consequent repentance and redemption). In the original sin of "Eve," the mother of all humanity, in that original sin, committed in the "youth" of humankind, we see our own sins, as we pray in the words of this Psalm: "The sins of my youth and my ignorance remember not; according to Your mercy remember me, for the sake of Your goodness, O Lord" (Pss 24/25:7). And we celebrate God's granting of his law to humanity after our fall(s): "Good and upright is the Lord; therefore will He set a law for them that sin in the way" (Pss 24/25:8). In our time, in the era of the church, we do not understand this "law" to mean the Mosaic law, but the discipline that we embrace when we repent and make right our ways, after we've gone off track and "sinned" (or "missed the mark"). Our "law" or our *discipline*, by which we become *disciples*, is that of following the eternal Word of God, Jesus Christ, on the Way of the Cross that is our vocation. We resolve to follow this Way every time we get up from the rut of a sinful pattern and re-embrace the healthy "fear" that is the fear of the Lord: "Who is the man that fears the Lord? He will set him a law in the way which He has chosen. His soul shall dwell among good things, and his seed shall inherit the earth" (Pss 24/25:12–13). Thus we become truly productive through repentance, as were Adam and Eve in their God-given vocations after the fall (Gen 3:16–19), when they worked the soil and had children.

The third of the three psalms of the Third Hour, *Pss 50/51* ("Have mercy on me, O God, according to Your great mercy"), is placed within the Third Hour service for two reasons: 1. It reflects the penitential theme of *Eve's Tasting of the Forbidden Fruit* (and her consequent repentance and redemption), as described in the preceding paragraph, and 2. It is appropriate to the main theme of the Third Hour, which is *Pentecost* (or the descent of the Holy Spirit on the Apostles), because it mentions the Holy Spirit in three consecutive verses: "Create in me a clean heart, O God, and renew the right Spirit within me. Cast me not away from Your presence, and take not Your Holy Spirit from me. Restore unto me the joy of Your salvation, and with Your governing Spirit establish me" (Pss 50/51:10–12). Along with these appeals to God, for him to fill us, his church, with the Holy Spirit (as he filled the apostles at Pentecost), we also profess our faith in the teaching capacities of a Spirit-filled church. As we say in the next verse of this psalm: "I shall teach transgressors Your ways, and the ungodly shall return to You" (Pss 50/51:13). Further, we profess the capacities of a Spirit-filled church for praise and true worship, which comes from the "brokenness" of our cross-carrying Way: "O Lord, You shall open my lips, and my mouth shall declare Your praise. For if You had desired sacrifice, I had given it; with whole-burnt offerings You shall not be pleased. A sacrifice unto God is a broken spirit; a heart that is broken and humbled God will not despise" (Pss 50/51:15–17). Finally, toward the end of this Psalm, we profess our faith in God's kind of "building," in which he engages us as church or as "Sion," known in Byzantine hymnography as "the Mother of Churches": "Do good, O Lord, in Your good pleasure unto Sion, and let the walls of Jerusalem be built" (Pss 50/51:18). Thus, in the first part of our workday, at the Third Hour, we are reminded that all our "building" in and of the "new Jerusalem" that is the church, is based on God's grace, which flows abundantly into our broken and humble hearts.

How Can We Pray the Third Hour?

In modern-day Orthodox and Greek Catholic parishes, the Third Hour is either omitted altogether (in Greek Orthodox practice), or it is chanted together with the Sixth Hour, immediately before Divine Liturgy (in Russian, Ukrainian, and related traditions).[10] The faithful pay little attention to the Third and Sixth Hours, and most of them will arrive at church when the Hours are just about over, and the Divine Liturgy is beginning. The few parishioners who are in church during the chanting of the Third and Sixth Hours, apart from the reader who is chanting these Hours, are usually occupied with something *else*; the choir conductor is preparing the sheet-music for the upcoming Divine Liturgy (or perhaps even conducting a quick choir-rehearsal in the neighboring parish hall), the priest is celebrating the Proskomide or hearing confessions, several others may be buying or selling candles, and so on. As is the case with the First Hour, our present-day approach to the Third Hour prayer service, even though it is usually celebrated at its proper time (about 9 am), testifies to the fact that we do not quite "get" it.

How can we begin to rediscover the Third Hour? We can pray this Hour every day, simply by repeatedly chanting aloud, or saying to ourselves, its main Troparion-hymn, from about 9 am to about 12 noon. The Troparion of the Third Hour is a poetic composition that refers the Pentecost event, the descent of the Holy Spirit on the apostles, to our lives:

Third-Hour Troparion:

"O Lord, You sent Your most Holy Spirit upon Your Apostles/ at the third hour./ Take Him not from us, O Good One,// but renew us, who pray to You."

In between our repetition of the Troparion, we can insert verses from Pss 50/51 of the Third Hour, e.g.:

---

10. On Lenten weekdays, the Third Hour is chanted in a row with the other Little Hours, one after the other, following Matins in the morning.

Verses to Insert Between Repetitions
of the Third-Hour Troparion:

- *"Create in me a clean heart, O God, and renew the right Spirit within me."* (Pss 50/51:10)

- *"Cast me not away from Your presence, and take not Your Holy Spirit from me."* (Pss 50/51:11)

If we do not know these verses by heart, we could alternatively insert some other prayer that we do know, e.g.:

Other Prayers to Insert Between Repetitions
of the Third-Hour Troparion:

- (Jesus Prayer) *"Lord, Jesus Christ, Son of God, have mercy on me, the sinner."*

- *"Our Father . . ."*

- (To the Theotokos) *"Most Holy Theotokos, save us!"*

- (To the Saint of the Day) *"Holy (Martyr, Father, Mother, etc.) N, pray to God for us!"*

- (On Mondays) *"Holy Archangels and Angels, pray to God for us!"*[11]

- (On Tuesdays) *"Holy and Great John, Forerunner of the Lord, pray to God for us!"*

- (On Saturdays) *"All Saints, pray to God for us!"*

As in the case of the First Hour, it is important to keep our Third Hour prayer simple, so that it is doable and sustainable within a busy schedule. So, we don't overthink or over-complicate the way that we do it. On normal workdays we may have many distractions at this time, between 9 am and 12 noon, so we might only get to pray the Troparion just once or twice, in between phone calls, in between responding to emails or texts, in between or during classes if we are students or teachers, in between tending to patients if we

---

11. For more on the weekday-commemorations, see chapter 2.

are medical professionals, or while tending to some other responsibilities in the first half of our day. On some days, if we are new to praying the Hours in this way, we may forget to pray the Third Hour for most of its time-window (from 9 am to 12 noon). But even if we remember at around 11 am, or just before noon, we can still do it just briefly. If we forget the Third Hour entirely, and remember about prayer at around 1 or 2 pm, we can just get back on track, and proceed to pray the Sixth Hour, making a mental note to remember the Third Hour tomorrow. With practice, when we spend a week or two praying this way, we will develop an inner sort of prayer-clock, which will call us to pray the Hour at hand.

The way the Third Hour happens in my everyday life, in an apartment in the city-center of Vienna, Austria, is as follows. On weekdays, between 9 am and about 12 noon, I am usually still seated at my computer, preparing my weekday audio podcast and daily reflection (a brief reflection on a passage from Scripture), and then I am posting these online. So, I chant the full Troparion, "*O Lord, You sent Your most Holy Spirit upon Your Apostles . . .*" whenever I get up to get a refill of coffee or water, or when I pause from my work to look out the window. Sometimes I also just say the verses from Pss 50/51, "*Create in me a clean heart*" and "*Cast me not away,*" in the brief moments that I remember it is the Third Hour. On some days, I finish all my computer-related work well before noon, so I continue to say the Third-Hour Troparion and these verses during my next activity, which is about twenty-five minutes of strength exercises, done on a mat in my living-room. One can't easily say the Troparion and verses aloud during physical exertion, so during strenuous physical exercise I pray these in my mind. The Third-Hour Troparion is particularly helpful during both of my morning activities, the creative/intellectual kind (of writing and podcast-recording) and the physical kind (of strength-exercises), because in this prayer we call for the Holy Spirit, Who is the Giver of all kinds of strength and inspiration. This Troparion also grounds my various types of "work" in the Pentecost-event, which is known as "the birthday of the church." So, through praying in this way I am reminded that I am "working" within and thanks to the mystery that is the church, even if

I do not happen formally to be employed by the church, in the sense of getting paid by a church-parish or diocese.

THE SIXTH HOUR

The Sixth Hour prayer service, known in Western traditions as Sext, is meant to be celebrated at some point between about 12 noon and about 3 pm. Its main *theme*, or the motivation it offers us for prayer at this time of day, is our grateful remembrance of another important event of salvation history that happened at this time of day, *the Crucifixion*, or the nailing of Christ to the cross and his passion. We also remember the events that accompanied his passion, particularly the "darkness" that set "over all the land from the sixth hour to the ninth hour" (Matt 27:45 NKJV), and Christ's cry from the cross, "My God, My God, why have You forsaken Me?" (Matt 27:46 NKJV).

The symbolism of the "darkness" of this hour, midday, is accompanied with a symbolism of Divine "light," because the sun is usually at its brightest at midday. Hence the Sixth Hour is a time both of abundant grace and intense temptation; it is the time of "the noonday demon" mentioned in the Septuagint version of the third of the three psalms of the Sixth Hour, in Pss 90/91:6. In the more-sunny regions of the world, this Hour is one of rest, and already among the Jews it was considered most appropriate to (private) prayer. So, devout Jews would use this time of rest also for some private prayer, as did Saint Peter in Acts 10:9, when he "went up upon the housetop to pray about the sixth hour." Note that the term "siesta" comes from the Latin term for the Sixth Hour, "Sext," at which time, according to the Benedictine rule, monks could catch up on some sleep, having chanted the nighttime hours.

The three psalms of the Byzantine Sixth Hour, Pss 53/54, 54/55, and 90/91, bring together all these themes, of Christ's passion on the Cross at midday, and of the intensity of both "darkness" and "light" at this central time of our own day. Let us next take a look at these psalms, before discussing the main Troparion of the Sixth Hour and how we might pray it in the middle of our (work)day.

Pss 53/54, 54/55, and 90/91, of the Sixth Hour

We read the first of the three Psalms of the Sixth Hour, *Pss 53/54* ("O God, in Your name save me"), as expressing the voluntary suffering of our Lord on the Cross, as well as his cry to the Father, from the cross: "For strangers are risen up against me, and mighty men have sought after my soul. . . . Willingly shall I sacrifice unto You; I will confess Your name, O Lord, for it is good" (Pss 53/54:3a, 6). In the light of the latter verse, we see Christ's cry from the cross, "My God, My God, why have You forsaken Me?" (Matt 27:46), perhaps surprisingly, as a confession of God's "good" name. Why? Because the God Man, even in this most difficult moment of his human suffering, in which he willingly experiences the human rift between God and humanity, continues to profess the Father as "My" God, and continues to speak with him, even while expressing the rift he is feeling between God and humanity as we often do, as abandonment. When we pray this psalm in the middle of our day, sometimes in the midst of certain difficulties or conflicts, we are encouraged to continue speaking to God, even if only to say, "Where are You?" Thus we "willingly sacrifice unto him" by calling upon him, because doing so, calling his glorious name, is always "a sacrifice of praise." However dark our circumstances, we hand these over to him, we offer these to him, even if we do so in the form of a question, e.g., "Why?"

The second of the three psalms of the Sixth Hour, *Pss 54/55* ("Give ear, O God, unto my prayer, and disdain not my supplication"), is, similarly to the previous psalm, giving voice to Christ's suffering, including his being betrayed by his own. "And if he that hated me had spoken boastful words against me, I might have hid myself from him. But it was you, O man of like soul with me, my guide and my acquaintance, who enjoyed food together with me; in the house of God we walked in oneness of mind" (Pss 54/55:13–15). This psalm is also prayed at the Sixth Hour because, in the context of passion-related themes, it mentions the classic Judeo-Christian prayer times, "evening, morning, and midday": "I have cried unto God, and the Lord heard me. Evening, morning, and midday will I tell of it and will declare it, and He will hear my voice" (Pss 54/55:18–19). Even as we remember Christ's passion and prayer on his cross in the middle of our day, Pss 54/55 urges also each of us, on our cross-carrying journeys, to "Cast your care upon the Lord, and He will nourish you" (Pss 54/55:25a). We are nourished, rather than running on empty, when we sprinkle just a bit of hourly prayer throughout our daily schedules.

The third of the three psalms of the Sixth Hour, *Pss 90/91* ("He that dwells in the help of the Most High"), is chanted specifically at the Byzantine Sixth Hour service, because in its Greek (Septuagint) version this psalm mentions the "noonday demon":[12] "You shall not be afraid of the terror at night, nor of the arrow that flies by day, nor of the thing that walks in darkness, nor of the mishap and noonday demon" (Pss 90/91:5b–6). As mentioned above, the middle of the day, when the sun is at its most intense and brightest, is traditionally considered a time both of abundant grace and of intense temptations or trials. The "noonday demon," rendered in the Septuagint as *"daimoniou mesemvrinou,"* and in the 1611 King James Version according to the original Hebrew, "the destruction that wasteth at noonday," is thought in Christian ascetical literature to be a particularly vicious demon that attacks the ascetic in the middle of the day, causing despondency, restlessness, and an aversion to his or her own vocation. Succumbing to "the noonday demon" means slipping into despondency in the very middle of our workday and wasting time or abandoning our work altogether as a result, which can be understood as "the destruction that wasteth at noonday." Psalm 90/91 also includes the words with which the devil tried to tempt the Lord himself: "For He shall give His angels charge over you. . . . On their hands shall they bear you up, lest at any time you dash your foot against a stone" (Pss 90/91:11, cf. Matt 4:6). So, as we pray the Sixth Hour, if even just by chanting its main Troparion, addressed to Christ, we can also remember Heb 4:15 (NKJV): "For we do not have a High Priest who cannot sympathize with our weaknesses, but was in all points tempted as we are, yet without sin."

12. Scott-Macnab, "Noonday Demon."

How Can We Pray the Sixth Hour?

As in the case of the Third Hour, in modern-day Orthodox and Greek Catholic parishes the Sixth Hour is either omitted altogether (in Greek Orthodox practice), or it is chanted right after the Third Hour, immediately before Divine Liturgy (in Russian, Ukrainian, and related traditions).[13] This means that the Sixth Hour, if chanted at all, is chanted at about 9 or 10 am, and within the same twenty-five to thirty minutes as the Third Hour, which is the approximate time it takes to chant both these Hours. So, the Sixth Hour loses its intended purpose, which is to help us "redeem the time" of our midday. It is also lost to most of us, because most of us are either not in church yet, when the Third and Sixth Hours are chanted, as described above in our discussion of the Third Hour. It is understandable, for practical reasons, that there is no other time to chant the Sixth Hour, when the Typicon allocates it to the time just before the Divine Liturgy. But it clearly does not "work" here, because we, as church, are not "working" it. As with the other Hours, it seems we must find a different way of celebrating also the Sixth Hour.

How can we begin to "work" the Sixth Hour? We can pray this Hour every day, simply by repeatedly chanting aloud, or saying to ourselves, its main Troparion hymn, from about 12 noon to about 3 pm. The Troparion of the Sixth Hour is a poetic composition that refers the Lord's Crucifixion, which happened at the Sixth Hour and on the sixth day of the week (Friday), to our lives:

Sixth-Hour Troparion:

"On the sixth day and hour, O Christ God, / You nailed to the Cross / the sin which rebellious Adam committed in paradise./ Tear up also the report of our iniquity,// and save us!"

In between our repetition of the Troparion, we can insert verses from Pss 54/55 of the Sixth Hour, e.g.:

13. On Lenten weekdays, the Sixth Hour is chanted in a row with the other Little Hours, one after the other, following Matins in the morning.

Verses to Insert Between Repetitions
of the Sixth-Hour Troparion:

- *"Give ear, O God, unto my prayer, and disdain not my supplication."* (Ps 54/55:1)

- *"I have cried unto God, and the Lord heard me."* (Ps 54/55:18)

If we do not know these verses by heart, we could alternatively insert some other prayer that we do know, e.g.:

Other Prayers to Insert Between Repetitions
of the Sixth-Hour Troparion:

- (Jesus Prayer) *"Lord, Jesus Christ, Son of God, have mercy on me, the sinner."*

- *"Our Father. . ."*

- (To the Theotokos) *"Most Holy Theotokos, save us!"*

- (To the Saint of the Day) *"Holy* (Martyr, Father, Mother, etc.) *N, pray to God for us!"*

- (On Mondays) *"Holy Archangels and Angels, pray to God for us!"*[14]

- (On Tuesdays) *"Holy and Great John, Forerunner of the Lord, pray to God for us!"*

- (On Saturdays) *"All Saints, pray to God for us!"*

- (On Sundays) *"Glory be, O Lord, to Your holy resurrection!"*

As with the other daily Hours, it is important to keep our Sixth Hour prayer simple, so that we can do it in some way every day, between midday and about 3 pm, regardless of the circumstances. On normal workdays we probably have a lunchbreak at some point within these three hours, so we might pray the Troparion then, or while preparing or going to buy our lunch. And if we forgot about it then, but remember Sixth Hour prayer at around 2 pm, when we're

---

14. For more on the weekday commemorations, see chapter 2.

back to work, we can pray it then, perhaps with little prayers to the saint/s of the day or weekday in between. With practice, as mentioned before, we will develop an inner sort of prayer-clock, which will call us to pray the Hour at hand, even if our inner prayer-clock is sometimes slow or distracted, so it kicks in toward the end of the liturgical "Hour."

Sixth Hour prayer is particularly effective against our modern-day affliction of despondency, known as "the noonday demon" in ascetical literature. It is a sense of boredom with our vocation, or dissatisfaction with a perceived insufficiency of our vocation, whatever it happens to be. In the age of social media, when we are often painfully self-aware, and aware of what everyone else is doing, we easily get sucked into living a comparative life, comparing ourselves to those who are doing more or doing better, than are we. In the middle of our day, we might get bogged down with a sense of not doing enough of what we should be doing, or not enough of what we would like to be doing. The Troparion of the Sixth Hour gives voice to our list of "should haves" and "would haves," by calling this list "the report of our iniquity," which we hand over to Christ and ask him to "tear up" this list, and to "save us," or to return us to wholeness in him.

In my everyday life, I pray the Sixth Hour privately every day except Sundays, because on Sundays it is celebrated in church,— even though it is misplaced and makes little sense in our practice, as I complained above. But on days when I am not in church, between noon and 3 pm I usually do several things: I prepare and eat lunch, sometimes run an errand or two if I need to (go grocery-shopping, go to the post-office, etc.), and by 2 pm I take a forty-minute nap. While preparing lunch and also before the nap, I like to chant the Troparion aloud (I sing it in Slavonic and in the 2nd Tone, because that is what I am used to). Because I live alone it doesn't annoy anyone. While running errands, I often get distracted, but then I get the feeling that I'm missing something, and say some simple prayer to myself, usually the Jesus Prayer. But the Troparion of the Sixth Hour, when I'm chanting it or praying it in my mind, often gives me pause, because it is so rich theologically. Sometimes I have an "aha!" moment. For example, just recently this Troparion made me think of the violence of the event, of Jesus being nailed to the cross, and how this violence, our violence, which he absorbed and overcame, also "absorbs" the violence that my own sins inflict on me. This is what is meant by the words of the Troparion, "You nailed to the cross the sin which rebellious Adam committed," and it offers me great consolation, when my conscious is burdened with this or that sin. It is a great gift, the prayer of the Sixth Hour, when it breaks into the middle of the daily schedule in this way.

THE NINTH HOUR

The Ninth Hour prayer service, known in Western traditions as None, is meant to be celebrated at some point between about 3 pm and 6 pm. Its main *theme,* or the motivation it offers us for prayer at this time of day, is our grateful remembrance of another important event of salvation history that happened at this time of day, *Christ's Death on the Cross* and other moments of his passion, like the forgiveness of the penitent thief. The theme of the Ninth Hour overlaps somewhat with that of the Sixth Hour, because we remember also at the Ninth Hour the "darkness" that set "over all the land from the sixth hour to the ninth hour" (Matt 27:45 NKJV), and Christ's cry from the Cross, "My God, My God, why have You forsaken Me?" (Matt 27:46 NKJV).

In antiquity, along with being a time of prayer, the Ninth Hour or "Nones" was the time of wrapping up the work of the day, going to the baths and preparing for supper. The book of Acts explicitly mentions that in the early days of their apostolic mission, Peter and John went to the temple to pray at this Hour: "Now Peter and John went up into the temple at the ninth hour of prayer" (Acts 3:1). In later monastic traditions, the Ninth Hour becomes the final liturgical service of the daily cycle, for which the monastic community gathers upon completion of the workday. In monastic practice today it is attached to the evening-service of Vespers, which immediately follows the Ninth Hour and which begins the daily liturgical cycle of the next day. So, the Byzantine service of the Ninth Hour, along with the passion theme also thematizes the joy of *returning to church* after the workday, in its first two psalms, 83/84 and 84/85. For those of us who are not monastics, the Ninth Hour is also usually the final part of our workday and (if we do not work from home) the time we *return home*, to our "domestic church." Thus, both its themes, of *Christ's death on the cross* (and our death to sin) and of *returning to church* can tie in well with our lives, as described below.

Pss 83/84, 84/85, and 85/86, of the Ninth Hour

The first of the three psalms of the Ninth Hour, *Pss 83/84* ("How beloved are Your dwellings, O Lord of hosts) is prayed at this Hour, as mentioned above, because in monastic tradition it is the first of the evening-services, for which monastics *return to church* after the workday. The psalm expresses the joy of being in "the house of God," which all of us can understand to mean our own home, and/ or more essentially our Father's house that is communion with him. Our "return home" can be understood as our *repentance* toward the end of the day, as in the word used in the Hebrew Bible for repentance, "shub," which means "return." As we conclude our day's work and re-focus on God, once again, we rejoice in the refuge God offers us in his "dwelling place" or his loving mercy. "For the sparrow has found herself a house," we say of ourselves in this psalm, "and the turtledove a nest for herself where she may lay her young, even Your altars, O Lord of hosts, my King and my God. Blessed are they that dwell in Your house" (Pss 83/84:3–5a). This psalm also echoes the main theme of the Ninth Hour, of *Christ's death on the cross*, which was his "return home" to his Father, after the crucified Lord committed his Spirit into the Father's hands (Luke 23:46): "O Lord of hosts, hear my prayer; give ear, O God of Jacob. O God, our defender, behold, and look upon the face of Your anointed one" (Ps 83/84:8–9). In this context we also remember *our own death* at this time of day, both our daily "death" to our sinful ways of thinking/ being or our "carnal mind," and the physical death at the end of our earthly life. We express hope that at that point even we will find a place in the "house of God," as we find it already here in the church, because we choose to return to him, again and again, even though we realize we are as "outcasts" or outsiders amongst the saints of the church. In this way, we embrace the attitude of the penitent thief on his cross: "I have chosen rather to be an outcast in the house of my God than to dwell in the tents of sinners. For the Lord loves mercy and truth, God will give grace and glory" (Pss 83/84:11–12a).

The second of the three psalms of the Ninth Hour, *Pss 84/85* ("You have been favorable/gracious, Lord, to Your land; You have returned the captivity of Jacob"), penitential in character, similarly thematizes the "return" of the "land" that is our hearts, as Saint Athanasius interprets the word "land" in this psalm,[15] to God. In this psalm we both celebrate God's "return" from his "anger," and ask him to return us, from our "captivity" (to our sinful patterns and addictions), as he returned the chosen people from Babylonian captivity: "You ceased all Your wrath, You have returned from the wrath of Your anger. Return us, O God of our salvation" (Pss 84/85:3–4a). As we "re-turn" to, or "re-focus" on the Lord's cross toward the end of our workday, we also gratefully celebrate the "mercy and truth" that came together in the God-Man and in his salvific death, overcoming the rift between God and humanity, as signified by the tearing in two of the temple curtain (Matt 27:50–51): "Mercy and truth have met together, righteousness and peace have kissed each other. Truth has sprung up out of the earth, and righteousness has looked down from heaven" (Ps 84/85:10–11). It is both by God's "mercy" and his nonnegotiable "truth," these two poles of his way of revealing himself to us, that we are "returned home," again and again, to him.

The third of the three psalms of the Ninth Hour, *Pss 85/86* ("Bow down Your ear, O Lord, and hear me, for I am poor and needy"), reflects the passion-theme of this Hour: "In the day of my affliction I cried unto You. . . . O God, transgressors have risen up against me, and the assembly of the mighty has sought after my soul" (Pss 85/86:6a, 13). This psalm also anticipates the "sign" of the resurrection: "Work in me a sign unto good, and let them that hate me behold and be put to shame" (Pss 85/86:16). When we read this psalm, we understand the "transgressors" and "them that hate" us as our own darker tendencies, which we are confessing to God

15. Athanasius, "Tolkovanija na psalmy," 280.

and saying, You take care of them. As always when we read about "the bad guys" in Holy Scripture, we do not divorce ourselves from them, just as our Lord chose to be numbered amongst criminals when he was willingly crucified amidst two of them. The aggressive or even violent tone of the psalms (and church hymnography) with regard to these "bad guys" is meant to encourage in us the kind of "violence" against our vices that Christ says is necessary to claim the kingdom of heaven (Matt 11:12 NKJV). As for the violence we commit against ourselves and one another, he willfully subjects himself to it on the cross, he literally "nails it," absorbing it and then overcoming it in his resurrection. We celebrate this life-bringing truth both in the main Troparia of the Sixth Hour and also of the Ninth Hour, to which we will turn next.

How Can We Pray the Ninth Hour?

In modern-day Orthodox and Greek Catholic parishes, the Ninth Hour is usually not celebrated. If ever celebrated at a parish, it is celebrated only during Lent, and/or (with different psalms and hymns) at the service of the Royal/Great Hours, celebrated three times a year.[16] In both cases, during Lent and at the Royal/Great Hours, it is usually chanted in the morning, in a row with the other Hours. On the rare occasion that the Lenten (vesperal) Liturgy of Presanctified Gifts is celebrated in the evening, at some parishes the Ninth Hour is chanted right before Vespers and the Presanctified liturgy, at about 6 or 7 pm. Never, to my knowledge, is the Ninth Hour chanted at its proper time, between 3 and 6 pm, not even on Holy and Great Friday.

Nonetheless, we could pray this Hour every day, along with the other Little Hours, simply by repeatedly chanting aloud, or saying to ourselves, its main Troparion hymn, from about 3 pm and about 6 pm. The Troparion of the Ninth Hour is a poetic composition that refers the Lord's death on the cross, which happened at the

16. The Royal or Great Hours are celebrated in the morning on the eves of Christmas and Theophany, and in the morning of Great Friday. In the latter case, on Great Friday, to have the Ninth Hour chanted in the morning makes the least sense.

Ninth Hour, to the kind of "death" we want to die every day on our cross-carrying journeys:

Ninth-Hour Troparion:

"*At the ninth hour, O Christ God,/ You tasted death in the flesh for our sake:/ mortify our carnal mind // and save us!*"

In between our repetition of the Troparion, we can insert the verses from Pss 118/119, which are traditionally inserted in between its repetition in the Horologion. Psalm 118/119 is chanted at the Byzantine funeral service, so its verses are selected for this Hour of the Lord's death:

Verses to Insert Between Repetitions of the Ninth-Hour Troparion:

- "*May my prayer come near before You, O Lord, according to Your word give me understanding.*" (Pss 118/119:169)

- "*May my petition come before You, O Lord, according to Your word deliver me.*" (Pss 118/119:170)

If we do not know these verses by heart, we could alternatively insert some other prayer that we do know, e.g.:

Other Prayers to Insert Between Repetitions of the Ninth-Hour Troparion:

- (Jesus Prayer) "*Lord, Jesus Christ, Son of God, have mercy on me, the sinner.*"

- (Penitent Thief Prayer) "*Remember me, O Lord, when You come into Your kingdom!*"

- "*Our Father . . .*"

- (To the Theotokos) "*Most Holy Theotokos, save us!*"

- (To the Saint of the Day) *"Holy* (Martyr, Father, Mother, etc.) *N, pray to God for us!"*

- (On Mondays) *"Holy Archangels and Angels, pray to God for us!"*[17]

- (On Tuesdays) *"Holy and Great John, Forerunner of the Lord, pray to God for us!"*

- (On Wednesdays and Fridays) *"Glory be, O Lord, to Your honorable Cross!"*

- (On Saturdays) *"All Saints, pray to God for us!"*

- (On Sundays) *"Glory be, O Lord, to Your holy resurrection!"*

As with the other daily Hours, it is important to keep our Ninth-Hour prayer simple, so that we can do it in some way every day, between about 3 and 6 pm, regardless of the circumstances. At this time on normal workdays, we probably complete our day's work, drive home from work or take the bus/train, perhaps go to the grocery store, meet with friends for drinks or dinner, or prepare dinner at home, etc. If we are constantly with other people between 3 and 6 pm, we might simply pray quietly, when we remember, the Penitent Thief Prayer, *"Remember me, O Lord, when You come into Your kingdom!"* It's more of a fulfilling adventure, however, to actually pray the Troparion, *"At the ninth hour, O Christ God,"* because then we name the hour at hand, we become present to this time of day, in a way that makes us present to the Lord's death on the cross two thousand years ago. It is especially refreshing if we are tired and despondent toward the end of our day, when we might feel like doing nothing but spacing out and watching Netflix or YouTube. This is not to dismiss our need for spacing out at the end of a long day, but it is helpful to temper our "spacing out" with just a bit of prayer.

In my everyday life, between 3 and 6 pm, I usually do the following: I have recently got up from my nap and have made tea or a decaf coffee, and I feel a bit less productive than in the morning. I suspect "the noonday demon" comes late to my apartment, having visited more worthy opponents at midday. The reader might

17. For more on the weekday commemorations, see chapter 2.

be thinking it is the decaf coffee, I know, but I prefer to suspect the noonday demon. Be that as it may, by 3 pm I am again sitting at my computer, and I do some writing, and I check social media and emails in case there is anything to which I need to respond. I chant the Troparion aloud (in Slavonic, and in the 8th Stichera Tone), in between things, and when I am preparing dinner at around 5:30 pm. I find the part, "mortify our carnal mind," particularly sobering, because when I am tired toward the end of the day, the darker parts of my "mind," like laziness and idleness, start to drag me down, and I feel like doing something useless, like watching the news or some political commentary on YouTube. On some days these issues do not come up, as I may have a meeting or a course to teach (all online, since the COVID pandemic), or some webinar. The verse of Pss 118/119, the first one, "*May my prayer come near before You, O Lord, according to Your word give me understanding,*" I especially cherish, because I always need better "understanding" when dealing with complicated theological topics in my line of work.

EVENING

The liturgical Hour of *Evening*, which begins whenever the sun sets, is not one of the "little" Hours; its liturgical service is Vespers (*esperinos* in Greek and *vechernya* in Slavonic), which is one of the two "big" Hours, together with Matins. It is included here, along with the "little" Hours, because this book would not be complete without at least some discussion of why and how busy people might find ways to integrate prayer also into the end of their day. Evening prayer is particularly challenging, when we are tired and perhaps only too happy to rest our bodies and minds in front of an iPhone or other screen, wineglass in hand. Not to disparage our need for rest, but when we go down the rabbit hole of watching or reading something like YouTube or Netflix, in which one video or story easily leads to another, we might sabotage our need for rest by overdoing it with our screentime. Some prayer discipline in our evenings can help us to put ourselves *and our phones/computers* to bed on time, for a healthier start to our next day.

Evening as the Beginning of the Next Day

Our prayer tradition is especially helpful in this regard, because it treats the evening as the beginning of our next day, and not as the end of the present one. According to Christian tradition, a day begins in the evening. This is because of the biblical creation narrative, which mentions "evening" first: *"So the evening and the morning were the first day"* (Gen 1:5b NKJV). So, the cycle of daily church services begins with Vespers, which celebrate the saint or feast of the next day. For example, on Monday evenings at Vespers, the hymns of the Octoechos are dedicated to the Tuesday commemoration of Saint John the Baptist. Learning to approach each evening not as an "ending" (of today) but as a "beginning" (of tomorrow) is one of the ways in which we might heal bad evening-habits that sabotage our nighttime "rest," both in the physical and spiritual sense.

Putting Our Phone/Computer "to Bed" in the Evening

Speaking of "bad evening habits," let me address the biggest and "baddest" of them all, before we discuss the main themes and prayers of Vespers. I'm referring to watching or scrolling through social media or other content in our phones or other electronic devices, often way past our bedtime. For those readers who are plagued by this particular "evening demon," more destructive to our generation than was the "noonday demon" to previous ones, I would suggest waging all-out, uncompromising war against him. Why?

In our twenty-four-seven Internet age we find ourselves in a world of ubiquitous electric lights and screens, which we find increasingly difficult to turn off, even at night. Our manmade technologies, when not employed with the gentle discipline of God's word and wisdom, are destructive to our capacities as human beings both to work and to rest in a healthy and timely manner. Here is how evolutionary biologists Heather Heying and Bret Weinstein describe our natural, human "biological clock" that to the minds of these secular authors until recently was "the only important parameter" that delineated our productive and dormant periods, according to the light and darkness periods of the natural world:

Tucked deep in our brains is a region called the supra-chiasmatic nucleus, which acts as our biological clock. It keeps track of what time of day it is—not in the sense of "5:00 p.m.," but in the sense of where we are with respect to photoperiod, the length of time in a twenty-four-hour period during which there is light—*because that was, until very recently, the only important parameter.* In London, 4:00 p.m. is called daytime in both December and June, even though in June the sun is still high in the sky at 4:00 p.m., whereas in December the sun has already set. Until recently, darkness mattered far more than one's position in a twenty-four-hour day. So we humans have done the expedient thing. We've used ingenuity to extend our productive period, by inventing artificial light. The benefits of this are obvious, but the hazards aren't. Before electric lights were invented, humans never experienced light after sunset of the intensity or duration that we are now commonly exposed to in our indoor spaces. . . . While daylight is bright and tends toward the blue end of the visible spectrum, and moonlight and firelight are dim and tend toward the red end of the spectrum, indoor lighting is typically brighter than either moonlight or firelight, and far bluer than, but not as bright as, daylight. This has the potential to interfere with circadian rhythms and hormonal cycles, and therefore to cause sleep disruptions.[18]

Nonetheless, present-day Christians have traditional tools at their disposal, aside from the "biological clock" in our brains, to tell us what time of day it is. We have the traditional prayer times, including the morning and evening Hours that lead us into the first light of day (as does The First Hour) and into the evening's sunset, as does Vespers or our evening prayer. Our church tradition provides us with these times and ways to "hallow" our resting periods on a daily basis. It is a gentle *discipline* that helps us become *disciples* of Jesus Christ, not missing out on the true "rest" he promises us in communion with him, and in him with one another. True rest evades us even in our beds, we might find, if we attach ourselves too heavily to the constant *"connectivity"* offered by our mobile phones,

18. Heying and Weinstein, *Hunter-Gatherer's Guide*, 98–99. Italics mine.

and to the detriment of *communion* with God and one another as offered to us in Christ, in the prayer tradition(s) and times of the church. Whether we are single or married, using our phones at night, when in bed, leads to a modern kind of loneliness, which seeks to "connect" with everyone and everything "elsewhere," rather than with the One and/or the one (i.e., our spouse, if we are married), whom we neglect while engrossed in our phone. In very practical terms, to be "redeemers of the time" in the twenty-first century, we are called to learn how and when to turn off our lights and screens, allowing ourselves (and others!) to "rest" according to God's Sabbath commandment, not abolished but fulfilled and expanded in the era of the church, to every day.

Here are some strategies or lifehacks, practical, spiritual, and psychological, for taming the "evening demon" that drags us by our fingertips to our phones at night. These are no more and no less than suggestions, not for everybody, but for anybody who feels plagued, rather than blessed, by nighttime phone-use:

1. Turn off the phone at least half an hour before bedtime, and leave it in another room, not your bedroom, until at least one half-hour after you wake up in the morning. When I turn off my phone at about 8:30 pm, I read the Prayer of Saint Simeon (Luke 2:29–32 NKJV, *Nyn apolyeis* in Greek, and *Nyne otpush-chaeshi* in Slavonic). I also put it in a pouch, which I call the phone's "sleeping bag." It is handmade and has a cross embroidered on it.

2. Avoid using your phone for your evening prayer routine (however brief or long) if this tends to tempt you to continue to use your phone past your bedtime. That is to say, don't depend on an app or texts in your phone; use a prayer book instead, if you read the Evening Prayers of the Prayer Book. Or learn a brief Vespers hymn or verse by heart (see the list of these hymns and verses at the end of this section) and repeat this in your evening as described below. Writing it down on a Post-it and putting that on your bedside table will help to learn it by heart.

3. If you are plagued by thoughts of possible emergencies that might happen at night, and of which you might be notified via

your phone, ask yourself: When was the last time you were notified at night, via your phone, of such an emergency? Would
it have changed anything, were you to have found out in the
morning? And, what did we all do in such cases, before we had
mobile phones?

4. Do not despair or give up on evening prayer entirely, if/when
you slip, staying up late into the night with your nose in your
phone for no good reason. Tomorrow is another day and another evening, when God willing, we will have the chance to
do better. When I find myself having slipped in this way, late
at night, I say something like, "Ugh. Lord, forgive me, I have
been stupid. Remember me, Lord, when You come into Your
kingdom!" Or if I feel really bad, I might say my really des-
perate prayer, "Lord, I have cried unto You. Hear me!" Then I
shut off my phone, handing myself over into God's mercy, and
go to sleep. I'll note here that I think it's very important that
we keep talking to God, even when we completely lose focus,
because that keeps us breathing, so to say, even when we feel
close to (spiritual) death. God wants us continuously to stay
in touch with him, even when we are down, just like a first
responder bends over a barely conscious person who has been
in an accident, saying, "Keep talking to me! Look at me! Keep
talking to me!"

Again, none-of-the-above is intended to burden those readers who need to use their phones in bed. It is intended for anyone
whose evenings (and mornings) would become easier, not more
difficult, by abstaining from nighttime phone use.

The Main Themes & Prayers of Vespers

The main themes and corresponding prayers of Byzantine Vespers,
alongside the saint/feast of the next day, are:

1. Creation, or praising God for his creation, which began in
the evening as mentioned above. Corresponding prayer: Ps

103/104, "Bless the Lord, O my soul; O Lord my God, You have been magnified exceedingly."

2. Evening-light, both of sunset and other sources of light that we use in the evening. Corresponding prayer: "O Gladsome Light" (*Fos ilaron* in Greek, *Svete tikhiy* in Slavonic).

3. The "fall" of Adam and ensuing repentance. Corresponding prayers: Pss 140/141, "Lord, I have cried unto You, hear me," and the prayer, "Vouchsafe, O Lord, to keep us this evening without sin" (*Kataxioson, Kyrie* in Greek, and *Spodobi, Gospodi* in Slavonic).

4. Salvation and true rest coming through Jesus Christ. Corresponding prayer: The Prayer or Song of Simeon from Luke 2:29–32 (*Nyn apolyeis* in Greek, and *Nyne otpushchaeshi* in Slavonic).

How Can We Pray in the Evening?

Given what we noted earlier about the "Prayer Book" (*Molitvoslov*) replacing the traditional Hours, rather than the "Evening Prayers" we might choose a psalm verse and/or a hymn from those mentioned above (the texts or incipits of which are provided below), and repeat it to ourselves in our evenings, from 6 pm until we turn off our phone and computer and go to bed.

The following is a list of brief prayers or psalm verses from Byzantine Vespers, to repeat (aloud or to ourselves) in our evening:

BRIEF EVENING PRAYERS AND VERSES:

- *"Bless the Lord, O my soul; O Lord my God, You have been magnified exceedingly!"* (Pss 103/104:1)

- *"Lord, I have cried unto You, hear me."* (Pss 140/141:1)

- *"O Gladsome Light of the Holy Glory of the Immortal Father, Heavenly, Holy, Blessed Jesus Christ! Now that we have come to the setting of the sun and see the light of evening, we praise God Father, Son and Holy Spirit. For meet it is at all times to worship*

You with voices of praise. O Son of God and Giver of Life, therefore all the world does glorify You." (Byzantine Vespers Hymn)

- *"Vouchsafe, O Lord, to keep us this night without sin. Blessed are You, O Lord, the God of our Fathers, and praised and glorified is Your name unto the ages. Amen. Let Your mercy, O Lord, be upon us, as we have hoped in You. Blessed are You, O Lord, teach me Your statues. Blessed are You, O Master, grant me understanding of Your statutes. Blessed are You, O Holy One, enlighten me by Your statutes. O Lord, Your mercy endures forever; disdain not the works of Your hands. Unto You is due praise, unto You is due song, unto You glory is due, to the Father, and to the Son, and to the Holy Spirit, now and ever, and unto ages of ages. Amen."* (Byzantine Vespers Prayer)

EVENING PRAYER BEFORE
TURNING THE PHONE OFF:

"Lord, now You are letting Your servant depart in peace,
According to Your word;
For my eyes have seen Your salvation
Which You have prepared before the face of all peoples,
A light to bring revelation to the Gentiles,
And the glory of Your people Israel." (Prayer of Simeon, Luke 2:29–32)

Table 1: Troparia and Verses of the Hours

Hour	Theme(s)	Troparion	Verses
First Hour (Sunrise— 9am)	Morning, Morning Light (Sunrise)	*In the morning hear my voice, / my King and my God.*	*- Give ear to my words, O Lord; hear my cry.* *- For unto You will I pray, O Lord.* *- And let the brightness of the Lord our God be upon us, and the works of our hands do guide aright upon us, yea, the work of our hands do guide aright.*
Third Hour (9am—12 noon)	Pentecost, Descent of the Holy Spirit	*O Lord, You sent Your most Holy Spirit upon Your Apostles/ at the third hour./ Take Him not from us, O Good One,// but renew Him in us, who pray to You.*	*- Create in me a clean heart, O God, and renew the right Spirit within me.* *- Cast me not away from Your presence, and take not Your Holy Spirit from me.*
Sixth Hour (12 noon— 3pm)	The Crucifixion (the nailing of Christ to the Cross)	*On the sixth day and hour, O Christ God, / You nailed to the Cross / the sin which rebellious Adam committed in paradise./ Tear up also the report of our iniquity,// and save us!*	*- Give ear, O God, unto my prayer, and disdain not my supplication.* *- I have cried unto God, and the Lord heard me.*

Ninth Hour (3pm—6pm)	The Death of Christ on the Cross	*At the ninth hour, O Christ God,/ You tasted death in the flesh for our sake:/ mortify our carnal mind // and save us!*	- *May my prayer come near before You, O Lord, according to Your word give me understanding.* - *May my petition come before You, O Lord, according to Your word deliver me.*
Evening (6pm—Bedtime)	Creation, Evening Light (Sunset), The Fall & Redemption, True Rest	*Lord, now You are letting Your servant depart in peace, According to Your word; For my eyes have seen Your salvation Which You have prepared before the face of all peoples, A light to bring revelation to the Gentiles, And the glory of Your people Israel.*	- *Bless the Lord, O my soul; O Lord my God, You have been magnified exceedingly!* - *Lord, I have cried unto You, hear me.*

2

The Days of the Week

IN ADDITION TO THE hours of the day, the seven days of the week also each have their liturgical traditions and themes, expressed mainly in the Byzantine liturgical book that governs the weekdays, called the *Oktoechos* in Greek and *Oktoich* in Slavonic. The weekday commemorations shed additional light on our redemptive walk through time.

We think of the seven days of the week as "the seven pillars" on which Divine Wisdom builds her "house," as described in Prov 9:1-6. In this "house," which is the church within time, Wisdom serves us her "bread and wine" of knowledge not all at once, but bit by bit and day by day, within the seven-day structure of our time:

> Wisdom has built a house for herself, and set up seven pillars. She has killed her beasts; she has mingled her wine in a bowl, and prepared her table. She has sent forth her servants, calling with a loud proclamation to the feast, saying, Whosoever is foolish, let him turn aside to me: and to them that want understanding she says, Come, eat of my bread, and drink wine which I have mingled for you. Leave folly, that ye may reign forever; and seek wisdom, and improve understanding by knowledge (Prov 9:1-6 LXX).

In this chapter we will explore the meaning attached to each weekday in Scripture, liturgy, and everyday life, and see how these meanings can help us become more present to God, to time, and to all of creation, not only on Sundays.

Before we get to the Byzantine weekdays, here is just a bit of background information about the week in general. The seven-day week was observed by ancient Israel, according to the biblical account of creation in Gen 1.[1] In Hebrew, most weekdays are derived from ordinals, e.g., Sunday—"first day" (*yom rishon*), Monday—"second day" (*yom sheni*), etc., each reflecting the remembrance and theology of the respective days of creation. Then came the planetary week, with the weekdays named after the seven "planets" known to ancient peoples (including the sun and the moon), based on pagan astrological beliefs and deification of the planets. While the Jews counted their "days" from evening to evening (or sunset to sunset),[2] the ancient Greeks counted them from dawn to dawn and the Romans from midnight to midnight (as do we in our secular calendar). While it remains unclear why ancient peoples came to divide their time into seven-day units,[3] the number seven lends itself well to a Christian numerology, with one in its center (Wednesday), flanked equally by three. We will be returning to that numerology as we discuss each of the weekdays in the following pages.

Various Christian(ized) peoples and cultures have inherited both or either the Jewish and the planetary week in different ways, as reflected in their languages. For example, in modern Greek most of the weekdays are derived from ordinals, according to the Jewish count of the weekdays, e.g., Monday—"Second" (*Devtera*), Tuesday—"Third" (*Triti*), etc. But Sunday in Greek is "The Lord's (Day)" (*Kyriaki*), and Friday is "Preparation (Day)" (*Paraskevi*), for reasons that will be discussed below. In Russian and other Slavic languages, three of the seven weekdays are also derived from ordinals, but not according to the Jewish, Sunday-first count. In Russian, the "Second (Day)" is Tuesday (*vtor-nik*), the "Fourth (Day)" is

1. Rordorf, *Sunday*, 9.

2. The counting of a "day" from sunset to sunset is characteristic of cultures that follow a lunar calendar. Cf. Talley, *Liturgical Year*, 14.

3. As Rordorf notes, "there are no natural processes, like rotations of the stars, or here on earth, to be found with a periodicity of seven days." Rordorf, *Sunday*, 18, and see 19–24 for the various theories on this question.

Thursday (*chet-verg*), and the "Fifth (Day)" is Friday (*pyat-nitsa* or *pyat-ok* in Church Slavonic),[4] while Sunday is called "Resurrection" (*voskresenie*) and Wednesday—simply, "Middle" (*sreda*). In English, the weekdays are named after the Nordic deities that correspond to the Roman deities, and the deified "planets" that inspire the weekday-names of the Roman planetary week and of modern Romance languages: for example, "Tuesday" is named after the Germanic god Tiw, who corresponds in the *interpretatio germanica* to the Roman god Mars (hence Tuesday is *martedi* in Italian, *mardi* in French, etc.).

Today, as in previous times, the different weekday counts and names within one and the same church, in the various liturgical languages of local Churches, do not rival one another but exist side-by-side. Note that this difference testifies to the tolerated and hence tolerable, also in the Orthodox Church, *changeability* of that part of Tradition that is keeping time. As in the case of the change from the sundial to the mechanical clock, the still extant *changes* brought to weekday names through their translation from the original language of the Byzantine Rite, Greek, to other liturgical languages within the Orthodox Church are more consequential than the difference of thirteen days between the Julian and Gregorian Calendars. Here we have a weekly, year-round difference in the theological significance of each weekday, insofar as its different names and the theological implications of those names go.

What brings together the experience of the different weekday names amongst the various local Churches, regardless of their meanings in local liturgical languages, is the commemoration attached to each day within one-and-the-same Byzantine liturgical Rite. Here are the commemorations attached to each day of the week according to the Byzantine liturgical book, the *Oktoechos*, which governs the weekly liturgical cycle:

- Sunday—The Resurrection
- Monday—The Angels and all Bodiless Powers
- Tuesday—Saint John the Baptist

4. Although Friday is called the "Fifth (Day)" in Church Slavonic, in the Sixth-Hour Troparion we still call it the "sixth" day: "On the sixth day and hour . . . (*Izhe v shestyj den' zhe i chas . . .*)."

- Wednesday—The Cross and Theotokos
- Thursday—The Apostles and Saint Nicholas
- Friday—The Cross and Theotokos
- Saturday—The Departed and All Saints

None of these commemorations appear to refer to the days of creation, as described at the beginning of the Bible. But a closer look at the Byzantine liturgical week reveals that it does re-present to us, and makes us present to, salvation history from its very beginning at creation to its future fulfilment. In what follows we will discuss the meaning of each day, and the simple ways in which we can live and pray these meanings on the days when we are usually not in church.

MONDAY

Monday (from the Anglo-Saxon word *mondandaeg* or "the moon's day"), dedicated in pagan cultures to the moon goddess, Luna, is called "dies Lunae" or "the day of the moon" in Latin and related languages, e.g., *lundi* in French and *lunedi* in Italian. In the Byzantine Rite it is the Day of the Angels and all Bodiless Powers. In Hebrew and in Greek it is called the second day (*yom sheni, Devtera*), differently from Slavic languages that consider Tuesday, not Monday, The second day (as in the Russian word for Tuesday, *vtornik*).

Monday as the Second Day, and the Day of the Angels

Why do we celebrate the Angels on Monday, which is the second day (or the first day in some languages)? The simple answer is, because in ancient and later rabbinic Judaism and in the ancient church there was a widely held belief that they were created either before everything else, on Day One of creation (when the "first heaven" was created), or on the second day (when the "second heaven" of the firmament was created). The Bible leaves no doubt that the bodiless powers were indeed created by God, as stated in Ps 148:1, 5:

"Praise Him, all His angels: Praise Him, all His hosts. . . . Let them praise the name of the Lord: for He spoke, and they were made; He commanded, and they were created." However, because the Genesis creation story in the beginning of the Bible does not mention the creation of the angels, there were varying opinions on when, exactly, God created them.[5] But everyone agreed, as John of Damascus summarizes the issue in his *Exact Exposition of the Orthodox Faith* (2.3), that they were created before the human being.[6]

Our celebration of the angels on Mondays, then, links the beginning of our workweek to the very beginning of God's "work" of creating the world, specifically its invisible creatures. Our celebration of the angels every Monday also fortifies the faith we profess at the beginning of the Creed, our faith in One God as Creator of all things, visible "and invisible." Whether we associate Monday with Day One of creation or the second day, by "remembering" the earliest phase of creation we also connect with a timeless dimension of God's creative work, before the fourth day, when God created the planets "for signs and seasons, and for days and years" (Gen 1:14 NKJV), which meant the beginning of time. This is one of the ways in which the church's timekeeping, our timekeeping, occasionally dips a toe into that incomprehensible realm that is eternity.

The very idea of "celebrating" Mondays is rather countercultural, in those parts of the world where a Monday means resuming work. But when we wake up on a Monday, we are given to become more awake to the invisible "good guys" in our midst, the angels, including our very own guardian angel, and to befriend these "good guys" through prayer. By doing so, we also make known our choice, not to befriend the invisible "bad guys" in this world, who might instill in us feelings of dread, anxiety, and other kinds of darkness at our waking moment.

5. For more on the question of when the angels were created, see Osborne, *Cosmic Liturgy*, 21–24.

6. John of Damascus, *Polnoe sobranie tvorenij*, 191.

How Can We Pray on Mondays?

A simple way prayerfully to become present to a Monday, for those of us who do not attend daily church-services, is to insert a brief prayer to the angels and archangels in between the Troparion of every "Hour." (See the previous chapter, on Praying the Hours). For example, when we wake up and begin to pray the First-Hour Troparion, "*In the morning hear my voice, my King and my God*," we can say in between the repetitions of the Troparion:

- "*Holy Archangels and Angels, pray to God for us!*"
- "*Holy Angel of God, my Guardian, pray to God for me, the sinner!*"

We also continue to insert the psalm verses of the First Hour, or (if we don't know these by heart), other simple prayers, like the Jesus Prayer and/or the Our Father, or something else. And we do the same when the Third Hour rolls around, at about 9 am (or an hour or two later, when we happen to remember that it's the Third Hour), after we pray the Troparion, "*O Lord, You sent Your most Holy Spirit upon Your Apostles*," we can insert once or twice after this Troparion a brief prayer to the archangels and angels, and to our guardian angel. As mentioned in the previous chapter about this whole business of informal, hourly prayer, we keep things simple, and don't overcomplicate matters or stress out, if we don't get this "right." This is not some kind of obligation, about which we need to feel guilty, if we start doing it and then on some days forget about it. It is rather a tool or instrument, in the treasure chest of tradition, which we can pick up at any time, in our God-given freedom, as an aid in our dignifying challenge to "redeem the time."

TUESDAY

Tuesday (from the Old English word *Tiwesdaeg* or "day of Tiw"), named in English after Tiw, the Germanic god of war, is in the Byzantine Rite the day of Saint John the Baptist. Because the Germanic god Tiw is equated with the Roman god Mars, Tuesday (*dies Martis* in Latin) is named after Mars in the Romance languages, e.g., *Mardi* in French, *martedì* in Italian, etc. In Hebrew and in Greek it is called the third day (*yom shlishi*, *Triti*), while in Slavic languages it is the second day, as in the Russian word for Tuesday, *vtor-nik*. In Jewish folklore, Tuesday is considered a lucky day or "doubly blessed," because on the third day of creation God said "it was good" not once (as on the other days), but twice (Gen 1:10, 12b).

Tuesday as the Day of John the Baptist

Why do we celebrate Saint John the Baptist on Tuesdays? Tuesday is the day that immediately precedes the midpoint of the seven-day week, which is Wednesday. As such, it is a transitional or pivotal point to the week's center. Saint John the Baptist is also a transitional figure in salvation history, as the last and greatest of the prophets and Forerunner of the central figure, the incarnate Son of God. To celebrate Saint John the Baptist, the one who "prepares the way for the Lord" (Mark 1:3; Isa 40:3) in our hearts, means to reconnect with his message and his person. When we take pause on Tuesdays to hear once again the Forerunner's call to us to "repent" (to *change our mind* or *change our focus*), "for the kingdom of heaven is near" (Matt 3:2), it helps us to recharge our spiritual batteries and regain a sense of the "nearness" of the kingdom of heaven.

Celebrating Saint John the Baptist on "Tuesday," named in English and in most Romance languages after a pagan god of war (named "Tiw" in Germanic mythology or "Mars" in Roman mythology as mentioned above), also reminds us not to deify war or military aggression as did pagan cultures of various stripes. The ancient Greeks worshipped a war god called Ares, a fearsome and destructive deity, whose destabilizing power was meant to be kept at bay by offering him sacrifices. The Romans reinterpreted the character of Ares, identifying him with the Roman god Mars, whom they saw as representing military power that secured stability. The Romans also saw Mars as the father of the Roman people, although Mars and his offspring were not exactly "good guys" in our terms: in Roman mythology, Mars became the father of the twins Romulus and Remus, having raped the vestal virgin Rhea Silvia, who as a result became pregnant and gave birth to the twins. Romulus became the founder of the city of Rome, after killing his twin brother Remus. Thus, the cult of the Roman war god Mars, while viewing him as a "father" and as one who secured stability through military power, did not seem troubled by the rape and fratricide that feature prominently in the story of his family.

Our Christian hero, not a deity nor a product of our collective imagination, Saint John the Baptist, personifies a "violence" of a different kind:

> As they departed, Jesus began to say to the multitudes concerning John: "What did you go out into the wilderness to see? A reed shaken by the wind? But what did you go out to see? A man clothed in soft garments? Indeed, those who wear soft *clothing* are in kings' houses. But what did you go out to see? A prophet? Yes, I say to you, and more than a prophet. . . . And from the days of John the Baptist until now the kingdom of heaven suffers violence, and the violent take it by force." (Matt 11:7–9, 12 NKJV)

Saint John the Baptist exemplifies a "violence" that is a forceful, unambivalent decisiveness, to choose truth over falsehood, good over evil, and the kingdom of heaven over the kingdom(s) of men. This godly "violence" is not a murderous or destructive one; it is not inflicted on human beings or on any kingdoms of this world. It is a "violence" or force and decisiveness by which we are called to "take" the kingdom of heaven. This kind of Christian decisiveness has often sat uncomfortably with the kings and kingdoms, or emperors and empire-builders of this world, which is why a king imprisoned and beheaded Saint John the Baptist. The Forerunner of the Lord thus absorbed the ungodly violence of others, putting down his life, as do all the holy martyrs, bearing witness to the one thing needful. That's why, "from the days of John the Baptist until now" we are called to channel our God-given capacity for "violence" toward the only kind of warfare that is life-bringing and not death-bringing, the spiritual warfare. We are reminded of this every "Tuesday," named in English after a pagan god of war, but celebrated in our tradition in honor of Saint John the Baptist.

How Can We Pray on Tuesdays?

A simple way prayerfully to become present to a Tuesday, for those of us who do not attend daily church-services, is to insert a brief prayer to Saint John the Baptist in between the Troparion of every "Hour." (See the previous chapter, on Praying the Hours.) For example, when we wake up and begin to pray the First-Hour Troparion, "*In the morning hear my voice, my King and my God,*" we can say in between the repetitions of the Troparion: "*Holy and Great John, Forerunner of the Lord, pray to God for us!*"

We also continue to insert the psalm verses of the First Hour, or (if we don't know these by heart), other simple prayers, like the Jesus Prayer and/or the Our Father, or something else. We might be creative and insert a Gospel verse, e.g., "Repent, for the kingdom of heaven is at hand!" (Matt 3:2). But we don't want to overcomplicate our prayer routine with too much variety, lest it become too much and we drop it altogether.

WEDNESDAY

Wednesday (from the Old English word *Wodnesdaeg* or "day of Woden"), is named in English after Woden/Odin, the supreme Germanic god. In the Byzantine Rite it is the day of the "supreme" or central mysteries of Christianity, the cross and the Theotokos, and is usually a fast day. Because the supreme Germanic god Woden or Odin is equated with the supreme Roman god Mercury, Wednesday (*dies Mercurii* in Latin) is named after Mercury in the Romance languages, e.g., *mercredi* in French, *mercoledì* in Italian, etc. In Hebrew and in Greek it is called the fourth day (*yom ravi'i, Tetarti*); in Slavic languages it is not Wednesday but Thursday that is considered the "fourth" day (as in the Russian word for Thursday, *chetverg*), while Wednesday is simply called the Middle, as in the Russian *sreda*. In German, Wednesday is similarly called *Mittwoch*, meaning "mid-week."

Wednesday as a Day of the Cross and Theotokos

On Wednesdays we celebrate the cross and the Theotokos, just as we do on Fridays. Why do we celebrate the cross and the Theotokos on Wednesdays, in the center of the week? Because these are the central mysteries of Christianity, manifested in the "center" of salvation history. Just as the Sunday of the Cross is in the middle of Byzantine Lent, so is the cross planted in the center of our every week, along with the Theotokos, the "heavenly ladder" who brings together heaven and earth, manifesting the mysteries of both the incarnation and the mother church. It is from the vantage point of this "center" of history, from the incarnation and the cross (the earthly lifespan of Christ) that the church "reads" all of history; we read the Old Testament backwards, making "sense" of it in the light of Christ, and we also make sense of everything that happens after his redemptive works for us in their light. When we re-focus our attention on the cross and the Theotokos in the middle of our week, we also re-embrace our own vocation, as Christians, to go the way of the cross and the way of the Theotokos. She exemplifies the common vocation of all of us, as "Mother Church," to receive Christ, the Word of God, in our own "wombs," and then to share him or "give birth" to him in our own surroundings and in our own historical context. This is a "virgin birth" in the sense that we are empowered for this kind of "birth giving" or creativity not by any human being but by the Holy Spirit. Jesus pointed out this vocation that we share with his mother, when the woman cried out from the crowd and praised his mother, saying, "Blessed is the womb that bore you and the breasts which nursed you!" and he responded, "More than that, blessed are those who hear the word of God and keep it!" (Luke 11:27–28 NKJV). When we truly "hear" and internalize the Word of God, and "keep" him as he is, the one who emerged from the tomb, we share him and do not bury him, letting him emerge from the "tomb" (which becomes "womb") inside our own selves.

Wednesday is the day of the Theotokos not in a general sense, however, but specifically in the context of the cross. Hence the Wednesday hymns in honor of the Theotokos are called *stavro-theotokia* (cross-Theotokia, or *krestobogorodichny* in Slavonic) in the Byzantine liturgical books, thematizing the mother of God as one standing next to the cross; as one of us, as the mother church, standing next to the cross. We will reflect further on this point below, in our discussion of Friday and its stavrotheotokial hymns.

Wednesday as the Fourth Day

The "central" position of Wednesday, called the fourth day (in Hebrew and Greek) also reflects the meaning of the fourth day of creation, on which *time was formed*, as mentioned in the introduction to this book. *Time was formed* on the fourth day in the sense that God put certain things into motion, according to which all other motion could be "spanned, framed, and scaled."[7] As described in Gen 1:14–19, on the fourth day God created the "lights in the firmament" (and the sun, the moon, the stars, and planets), "for signs and seasons, and for days and years" (NKJV). This was part of the Creator's *ordering* of the universe, although there were as yet no other living beings, none of us, to *read* the "signs and seasons" created by him at this point. We were to be on the receiving end of the God-given "signs" of time, which we are to learn to read and celebrate to his greater glory. Wednesday is thus a "central" day in the sense that before it, God "worked" outside of time, and after it, he works within time and invites us to grow in knowledge of him through reading its "signs." In this sense, Wednesday or the fourth day is also the day that God enters into our time, having created it. This meaning of Wednesday reflects the theology both of the incarnation, of the Son of God stepping into our time, and of the cross, through which he accomplished the "work" of re-unifying him and humanity.[8]

---

7. "Time is not motion, but something about motion. *What* exactly about motion is it? *Time is the spanning, framing, and scaling of motion.*" Manchester, *Syntax of Time*, 90.

8. Cf. the tearing in two of the temple curtain when Jesus died (Matt 27:50–51a).

The Wednesday Fast

Why do we fast on Wednesdays? There is no simple answer to this question. The very first mention of Christians fasting on Wednesdays (and Fridays) is found in the early church order of the late first century, the *Didache*, which instructs its community of Christians to fast on Wednesdays and Fridays so as not to fast together with the non-Christian Jews, who fasted on Mondays and Thursdays: "And let not your fasting be with the hypocrites, for they fast on the second and the fifth day of the week; but do ye keep your fast on the fourth and on the preparation (the sixth) day" (*Did.* 8:1–2). According to the Didache, then, it's still a good thing for Christians to fast twice a week (for no specified reason), but it's not a good thing to do so with the non-believing Jews (called "hypocrites" here). So, as far as the Didache is concerned, Wednesdays and Fridays are chosen as our fast days for no reasons other than: 1. Christian identity-building, or distinguishing the church from the synagogue, at a time when the boundaries between the two were not yet all that clear, and 2. we do need to fast twice weekly (for no specified reason). One might speculate that "intermittent fasting," on two non-consecutive days of every week, was considered a healthy thing back then as it is now, in certain modern-day diets. Centuries later, the Wednesday fast is explained in reference to the betrayal of the Lord by "the council held by the Jews," as in Canon 15 of Archbishop Peter of Alexandria (+311): "No one shall find fault with us for observing Wednesday and Friday, on which we have been commanded to fast with good reason by tradition. On Wednesday owing to the council held by the Jews for the betrayal of the Lord; on Friday, owing to His having suffered for our sake."[9] A similar explanation for the Wednesday and Friday fast is offered in the *Apostolic Constitutions* V. 20 (ca. AD 380): "He commanded us to fast on Wednesday and Friday, on Wednesday on account of the betrayal, [and] on Friday on account of the passion."[10] One might add that fasting on the days of the cross, by which the Bridegroom was "taken from us," fulfills his words as to when his disciples will fast: "But the days will come

9. Agapis, *Rudder*, 754–55.

10. Grisbrooke, *Apostolic Constitutions*, 47.

when the bridegroom will be taken away from them; then they will fast in those days" (Luke 5:35 NKJV).

Regardless of the original reasons for the Wednesday fast, today it remains both a part of our identity, as Orthodox Christians, fostering our sense of belonging to a specific tradition, and also a way physically to participate in the Wednesday liturgical celebration of the cross. We "witness" to the passion theme of every Wednesday (and Friday) physically, by abstaining from animal products on these days, according to the fasting tradition of the Byzantine Rite. Our peculiar food choices or food limitations on Wednesdays are a symbolic act, testifying to the physical limitations of One nailed to a cross. Aside from being a healthy thing, this kind of weekly intermittent fasting from meat and dairy is also a way to draw us into the liturgical memory of Wednesdays (and Fridays) physically, because our tradition engages our whole being, not only its intellectual or "spiritual" side.

And please note that the traditional observation of Wednesdays, or any other days, either through fasting or praying, remains a tool or instrument of our tradition, which we either pick up and utilize to our benefit or don't, according to our circumstances and God-given freedom. The limitations placed on us through a fasting or prayer discipline are not chains or weapons, meant somehow to enslave us as would some tyrant. These limitations or guidelines of communal fasting and praying are offered to us as a frame, within which we can thrive as a community and as individuals within it, as does any work of art within its frame. Our tradition is a work of art, after all, within a frame(work) and within limitations that help us to thrive and realize our essence. As Chesterton famously said, "Art is limitation; the essence of every picture is the frame."[11]

How Can We Pray on Wednesdays?

There is a simple way prayerfully to become present to a Wednesday, in addition to being physically present to it by fasting. Those of us who do not attend daily church services can insert a brief prayer

11. Chesterton, *Orthodoxy*, 32.

of the cross and/or Theotokos in between the Troparion of every "Hour." (See the previous chapter, on Praying the Hours.) While the theme of the cross is already the dominant one in our Sixth and Ninth Hour prayers, every day of the week, on Wednesdays (and Fridays), we also insert it into our First and Third Hours. For example, when we wake up and begin to pray the First-Hour Troparion, *"In the morning hear my voice, my King and my God,"* we can say in between the repetitions of the Troparion:

- *"Glory be, O Lord, to Your honorable Cross!"*
- *"Most Holy Theotokos, save us!"*

We also continue to insert the psalm verses of each Hour, or (if we don't know these by heart), other simple prayers, like the Jesus Prayer and/or the Our Father, or something else. As for the prayers of the Sixth and Ninth Hours, they are already dedicated to the passion theme, as mentioned above, so we don't "need" to insert a special prayer of the cross. As on other weekdays, we don't want to overcomplicate our informal, hourly prayer routine with too much variety, lest it become too much and we drop it altogether.

THURSDAY

Thursday (from the Middle English word *Thuresday* or "Thor's day"), named after the Norse god of thunder, Thor, in the Byzantine Rite is the day of the apostles and Saint Nicholas. In Latin, Thursday was called *Iovis Dies*, after the Roman god of thunder and the sky, Jupiter, who was the Roman equivalent of Thor. In most Romance languages, Thursday is named after Jupiter, as in the Italian *giovedì*, the French *jeudi*, the Romanian *joi*, etc. In Hebrew and in Greek it is called the fifth day (*yom khamishi, Pempti*), differently from Slavic languages that consider Thursday the fourth day (as in the Russian word for Thursday, *chetverg*).

Thursday as the Day of the Apostles and Saint Nicholas

Why do we celebrate the apostles and Saint Nicholas on Thursday? Is there any connection with the fifth day of creation, on which God created the birds and creatures of the sea (Gen 1:20–23)? No, it is because of the theological chronology of salvation history, expressed in the structure of the Byzantine week. Just as Saint John the Baptist is celebrated on Tuesday as a transitional figure between Monday and Wednesday, which signify the beginning of creation (the angels) and the focal point of salvation history (the cross and incarnation) respectively, so are the apostles and a prominent successor to the apostles and participant in the First Ecumenical Council, Saint Nicholas, celebrated between Wednesday and Friday (the "preparation day" or "paraskevi" for Saturday), as transitional figures to the latter part of salvation history. Thursday is a transitional day from the middle of the week to its end, as the apostolic ministry facilitates the transition or *tradition* of Christ's salvific works into the era of the church. The church moves forward along the way of the cross, celebrated on Friday or *Paraskevi*, meaning "Preparation Day." The way of the cross is the "preparation" that leads us, as church, to the eternal Sabbath (Saturday). As we will see below, Saturday signifies the "end" of time, with its commemoration of the deceased and all saints. So, there is a certain chronological order to the weekday commemorations, albeit not exactly chrono-logical. The cross marks both the "center" of time in the middle of the week, on Wednesday, and also the way of "preparation" (or "paraskevi") for our eternal Sabbath.

One might expect Thursdays in Christian liturgical tradition to be eucharistic days, in memory of Great or "Maundy" Thursday,[12] the day of the Mystical/Last Supper. Just as all Fridays and Saturdays reflect the theology of Great Friday and Saturday, as we will see below, it would seem logical for Thursdays somehow to

---

12. The term "Maundy" Thursday comes from the Latin term "mandatum," meaning *commandment*, in reference to the Lord's words to his disciples at the Mystical Supper: "A new commandment I give to you, that you love one another: just as I have loved you, you also are to love one another" (John 13:34 NKJV).

commemorate Holy Thursday. The most obvious way to do that would be to celebrate the Eucharist on Thursdays, but neither the ancient Christians nor the Byzantines appear to have gone out of their way to gather for the Eucharist on Thursdays. It was always Sunday, and as the tradition developed, other days, e.g., Wednesday, Friday, and Saturday, that were the preferred days for the celebration of the Eucharist,—but not Thursday. The reasons for this curious fact are contested in liturgical scholarship and are beyond the scope of this little book.[13] But for our purposes, of walking through each weekday "with presence and meaning," our memory and celebration of the apostles every Thursday can also be inspired by Holy or Maundy Thursday. We'll return to that point shortly.

How Can We Pray on Thursdays?

We can prayerfully become present to a Thursday by inserting brief prayers to the Holy Apostles and Saint Nicholas in between the Troparion of every "Hour." (See the previous chapter, on Praying the Hours.) For example, when we wake up and begin to pray the First-Hour Troparion, "*In the morning hear my voice, my King and my God*," we can say in between the repetitions of the Troparion:

- "*Holy Apostles, pray to God for us!*"
- "*Holy Father Nicholas, pray to God for us!*"

We also continue to insert the psalm verses of each Hour, or (if we don't know these by heart) other simple prayers, like the Jesus Prayer and/or the Our Father, or something else. Note that in the case of the Third Hour, its Troparion is already dedicated to an "apostolic" theme, the descent of the Holy Spirit on the apostles or Pentecost: "*O Lord, You sent Your most Holy Spirit upon Your Apostles at the third hour. Take Him not from us, O Good One, but renew us, who pray to You.*" It is particularly appropriate to insert a brief prayer to the apostles after this Troparion, that they help us by their intercessions to take part in the ongoing Pentecost that is

13. Rordorf, *Sunday*, 225–35. See also Bradshaw, "Did Jesus Institute the Eucharist?," 1–19.

the life of the church. Our Thursday prayer to the Holy Apostles, particularly at the Third Hour, in a certain way also reconnects us with the central sacrament of the church, the Eucharist. We "remember" at this time the descent of the Holy Spirit "upon us, and upon these Gifts" that we offer to God at every Eucharist. When we "remember" the Eucharist or the Lord's Supper in this way, our every Thursday also becomes a remembrance and celebration of Holy and Great Thursday.

FRIDAY

"Friday," from the Old English word *Frigedaeg* or "Frigga's day," is named after the Germanic goddess of love, Frigga or Freia. This is because Frigga/Freia in the *interpretatio germanica* was associated with the Roman goddess of love, Venus, after whom this day of the week is named in Latin (*dies Veneris*) and related languages; e.g., *vendredì* in French, *vineri* in Romanian, etc. It is the "sixth day" in biblical and modern Hebrew (*yom shishi*). In Portuguese, different from other Romance languages Friday is called *Sexta-feira*, meaning "sixth day of liturgical celebration," similar to a term used for Friday in Latin liturgical texts, *feria sexta*. In Greek, Friday is also the sixth day of the week, but it is named *Paraskevi*, meaning "Preparation Day." This name is inspired by the Jewish custom of "preparing" for the Sabbath rest (on Saturday) by doing all work necessary for the Sabbath celebration (cooking, cleaning, etc.) on Friday. In Slavic languages, Friday is the "fifth day," as in the Russian *pyat-nitsa*.

In the Byzantine Rite, Friday is the sixth day, as well as the Day of the Cross and the Theotokos. It is also a fast day, similar to Wednesday. It is the Day of the Cross, because Christ was crucified and died on the cross on a Friday. It is the Day of the Theotokos not in a general sense, but similar to her Wednesday celebration in the context of the cross. Let us reflect further on all these aspects of Friday, one by one.

Friday as the Day of the Cross and of "Preparation"

Every Friday is a remembrance and celebration of Holy and Great
Friday, because it was on this weekday immediately preceding the
Sabbath (Saturday) that Jesus Christ was crucified and died on a
cross about two millennia ago. The Greek name for Friday, *Paraskevi* or "Preparation Day," in its Christian understanding, signifies
that the Way of the Cross "prepares" or leads us into the kind of
Sabbath "rest" that Christ offers: "Take My yoke upon you and learn
from Me, for I am meek and humble in heart, and you will find *rest*
for your souls" (Matt 11:29, my translation). In other words, a Friday leads to a Saturday just as the Way of the Cross "prepares for"
or leads to rest; just as walking through things (rather than avoiding
them) leads to peace of mind and soul.

Friday as the Sixth Day

As the sixth day of the week according to the Greek and Hebrew
count, Friday also reminds us of the sixth day of creation, on which
God created the human being, male and female, after creating the
rest of the living creatures of the earth (Gen 1:24–31). The whole
human "project," begun on the sixth day of creation, is also "finished" or "made complete" ("*Teteleustai*" in John 19:30) on the sixth
day of the week, on Holy and Great Friday, when Christ took upon
himself all our incompleteness, letting it die and be buried in him,
so as to rise again as the "new" Adam on the third day. In other
words, it was on the sixth day that he "nailed to the cross the sin of
Adam," as it says in the Troparion of the Sixth Hour: "*On the sixth
day and hour, O Christ God, You nailed to the Cross the sin which
rebellious Adam committed in paradise. Tear up also the report of our
iniquity, and save us!*"

Why Is the Theotokos Celebrated on Fridays (and Wednesdays)?

The mother of God is celebrated on Fridays and Wednesdays as the mother of God and as the "mother church" (a vocation we all share with her, insofar as we are church), standing next to the cross, grieving, wondering, and looking toward the light of the resurrection. Hence the Friday and Wednesday hymns in honor of the Theotokos, called "stavro-theotokia" or "cross-theotokia" (or *krestobogorodichny* in Slavonic), refer both to the personal experience of the Most Holy Virgin on a hilltop just outside Jerusalem about two millennia ago, and to the experience(s) of every Christian who follows him on that Way of the Cross. We are called in these hymns to imitate the grieving-yet-faithful mother, who does not abandon him crucified:

> At the sight of her Son crucified, the Virgin lamented with tears in her eyes: O my sweetest Child and Lord: You were given bitter vinegar for Your pain and suffering. Now, as the righteous Judge, we await Your resurrection in all Your might and power." (Stavrotheotokion of the Oktoechos, Thursday-evening Vespers, Lord, I have cried, Tone 1)[14]

In a better-known example of a "Stavrotheotokion," not from a Friday-service but from Holy and Great Saturday, "Do not lament Me, O Mother" ("*Ne rydai Mene, Mati*" in Slavonic and "*Mi epodyrou mou Miter*" in Greek), Christ is also addressing all of us, as mother church. I refer to its incipit here in English, Slavonic, and Greek, because it is a Stavrotheotokion with which most Byzantine Rite faithful will be familiar in at least one of these languages. Here is its full text:

> Do not lament Me, O Mother, seeing Me in the tomb, a Son conceived in the womb without seed, for I shall arise and be glorified. And I shall exalt with eternal glory, as God, those who with faith and love magnify you. (Irmos 9, Canon of Holy and Great Saturday)

14. Archdiocese of Canada, *Oktoechos,* 45.

Here Christ is consoling not only his mother, but all of us, the mother church, as we "see" him in the tomb and lament him, and by doing so "magnify" with faith and love the mystery of the faithful and loving church. He consoles us, even while he is the one who has suffered and died on the cross, as one who loves us and is taking care of us, even in his darkest hour, when he is descending into our hell.

Repentance and Fasting on Fridays

Speaking of the crucified Lord "taking care of us" on our cross-carrying journeys, on Fridays we also see ourselves as the penitent thief, received into paradise while crucified aside Christ. Even while our vocation, as church, overlaps with the cross-carrying vocation of the mother of God as described above, it overlaps also with that of the "good" thief, whose story is rather different from hers. Similar to him we have little to offer our Lord, once we "repent" or change our focus and recognize him co-suffering in our midst. We address him as the "good thief," not with the demands of the "bad thief" (*Save yourself and us!* Luke 23:39), but with the request that he but "remember" us in his kingdom:

> When the good thief saw You, O Christ, the only fruitful vine, he was most clever, speaking softly with grace, and stole forgiveness of his ancient sins. Let us all make haste to do as he did, and cry out: Remember us also, O lover of mankind.[15]

As on Wednesdays, the penitential and passion themes of Fridays inspire the fasting discipline of this weekday. Fasting is a way of being "bound" or restricted in a small way as one crucified is. Just as one's movements are restricted when nailed to a cross, so are our food-choices and other behaviors when fasting. We voluntarily "bind" ourselves through fasting on Fridays, as an act both of penance and of remembrance or *anamnesis*. We fast as the penitent thief, and remember both him and the One crucified next to

15. Archdiocese of Canada, *Oktoechos*, 90.

him, by doing so. Our fasting on the days of the cross, by which the Bridegroom was "taken from us," also fulfils his words as to when his disciples will fast: "But the days will come when the bridegroom will be taken away from them; then they will fast in those days" (Luke 5:35 NKJV).

How Can We Pray on Fridays?

On Fridays we can pray the Hours as we do on Wednesdays, by inserting brief prayers of the cross and Theotokos in between the Troparia of every liturgical Hour. While the theme of the cross is already the dominant one in our Sixth and Ninth Hour prayers, every day of the week, on Fridays (as on Wednesdays) we also insert it into our First and Third Hours. For example, between about 9 and 12 in the morning, when we pray to ourselves or aloud the Third-Hour Troparion, "*O Lord, You sent Your most Holy Spirit upon Your Apostles at the third hour*," we can say in between the repetitions of the Troparion:

- "*Glory be, O Lord, to Your honorable cross!*"
- "*Most Holy Theotokos, save us!*"

We also continue to insert the psalm verses of each Hour, or (if we don't know these by heart), other simple prayers, like the Jesus Prayer and/or the Our Father, or something else. As for the prayers of the Sixth and Ninth Hours, as mentioned above they are already dedicated to the passion-theme, so we don't "need" to insert a special prayer of the cross.

SATURDAY

"Saturday" or "Saturn Day" (*Saturnis dies* in Latin) is named after the planet and deity Saturn, the Roman god of agriculture and abundance/wealth. In Judeo-Christian understanding, Saturday is the seventh and final day of the week, and in the Byzantine liturgical tradition it is always a semi-festal day on which strict fasting is prohibited (except on Holy and Great Saturday). It is also the day of all saints and of all the deceased. The commemoration on Saturdays of all saints and deceased, of those who passed on to eternal "rest," reflects the theology both of Holy and Great Saturday, on which Christ "rested" in the tomb, and of the seventh day of God's creation, on which the heavens and the earth were "finished" and "He rested" (*shabath* in Hebrew and *katepausen* in Greek) from all his work (Gen 2:1–2). The fact that God completed all his works on the seventh day inspires the biblical symbolism of the number seven, which signifies completion and plenitude (e.g., seven churches, seven angels, seven seals, etc., in the book of Revelation; the "seven demons" cast out of Mary Magdalene in Luke 8:2; the seven basketfuls from seven loaves in Matt 15). The commemoration of *all* saints and deceased on Saturdays is also inspired by this symbolism of the number seven.

Saturday was the first weekday to be named among the Greeks and Romans after a planet, long before a proper planetary week developed among them in the first to third centuries AD. The pagan Saturday always coincided with the Jewish Sabbath, suggesting a connection between Jewish observances of the Sabbath and the pagan custom of not working on Saturdays.[16] As Hellenistic, Greek-speaking Jews settled in cities throughout the Mediterranean Basin from the mid-second-century BC, their Sabbath rest may have influenced the pagans to observe Saturdays in a remarkably similar way, or at least reinforced pagan superstitions about working on Saturdays, stemming from the belief that Saturn was a maleficent planet.[17]

Today, in many languages the name for this weekday is inspired either by the Sabbath (*Shabbat* in Hebrew, from *shabath* meaning "he rested" as mentioned above, and *Savvato* in Greek) or by the planet/deity Saturn or its equivalents. Examples of the former include the Slavic *sub(b)ota/sabota/sobota*, Italian *sabato*, Spanish *sábado*, French *samedi*, and German *Samstag* (from Greek *sam-n-baton*). Examples of the latter, of the planet/deity Saturn inspiring the name of the weekday, include the English *Saturday*, the

16. In this section I rely largely on Rordorf, *Sunday*, 27–41.

17. Rordorf, *Sunday*, 29.

Japanese name for Saturday that is *doyobi* or "soil day" (connected to Saturn or *dosei*, meaning "soil star"), and the Indian *Shanivara* or "Day of Shani," a Vedic god associated with the planet Saturn. In several languages, Saturday is associated with washing or bathing, as in the Scandinavian *lördag, laurdag*, or *lørdag*, meaning "bathday," similar to the Finnish *lauantai* and Estonian *laupäev*.

The Sabbath Commandment in the Old Testament

The earliest versions of the biblical Sabbath commandment, Exod 34:21 and Exod 23:12, command rest from one's work on the seventh day. Exodus 34:21 provides no reason for the prohibition of work on the seventh day, merely saying: "Six days you shall work, but on the seventh day you shall rest; even in plowing time and in harvest time you shall rest" (NKJV). A reason is given in Exod 23:12, which is to provide rest/refreshment for one's servants and cattle: "Six days you shall do your work, and on the seventh day you shall rest, that your ox and your donkey may rest, and the son of your female servant and the stranger may be refreshed" (NKJV). This ethical and social motivation, to show consideration for one's dependents, is expanded in the later, post-exilic (from ca. 538 BC to AD 1) more "theologized" and "sacralized" versions of the Sabbath commandment found in Exod 20: 8-11 and Deut 5:12-15. In Exod 20:11, the human "keeping holy" of the Sabbath day is explicitly connected to God's rest and "hallowing" of this day on the seventh day of creation: "For *in* six days the LORD made the heavens and the earth, the sea, and all that *is* in them, and rested the seventh day. Therefore the LORD blessed the Sabbath day and hallowed it" (Exod 20:11 NKJV). In other words, the Lord God initially made the Sabbath holy, and now it is our job *to keep it holy*. The "keeping holy" is further motivated and theologized in the Sabbath-commandment of Deut 5:12-15:

> Observe the Sabbath day, to keep it holy, as the LORD your God commanded you. Six days you shall labor and do all your work, but the seventh day *is* the Sabbath of the LORD your God. *In it* you shall do no work: you, nor

your son, nor your daughter, nor your male servant, nor your female servant, nor your ox, nor your donkey, nor any of your cattle, nor your stranger who *is* within your gates, that your male servant and your female servant may rest as well as you. And remember that you were a slave in the land of Egypt, and the LORD your God brought you out from there by a mighty hand and by an outstretched arm; therefore the LORD your God commanded you to keep the Sabbath day. (NKJV)

Here the motivation for keeping the Sabbath is that both the social dependents of the Israelites and the Israelites themselves may rest. It is more explicitly "theologized," as in post-exilic Judaism, the Sabbath rest had increasingly become marked with ritualized worship as the "keeping holy" of the Sabbath day.[18] It also acquired more of an *identity-building function* for the Israelites, to whom alone among the nations the Sabbath-commandment was given,[19] and who are commanded here to remember who they once were, slaves; whence they came, from enslavement in the land of Egypt; and Who it was that brought them out from there, the Lord their God. It is important to keep all these aspects of the Old Testament Sabbath in mind, as we next take a look at its further expansion in the New Covenant, in the era of the church.

The Sabbath in Church Tradition

It is often presumed that in Christian tradition the Sabbath commandment was transferred from one weekday to another, from Saturday to Sunday, although nowhere did the Lord of the Sabbath command rest on Sundays specifically. Jesus Christ "fulfilled" the Sabbath commandment not by moving it to Sundays, but by expanding it to every day and hour. He offers us "rest" in him, not through external abstinence from this or that activity, but by following him (at work, at play, on weekdays and weekends, in whatever we happen to be doing) in his Spirit, on the way of the cross.

18. Rordorf, *Sunday*, 17–18.
19. Rordorf, *Sunday*, 51.

He says to all who take up the "yoke" and "burden" of the cross, not only on Saturdays or Sundays:

> Come to Me, all *you* who labor and are heavy laden, and I will give you rest (*anapauso ymas*). Take My yoke upon you and learn from Me, for I am meek and humble in heart, and you will find rest (*anapausin*) for your souls. For My yoke *is* easy and My burden is light. (Matt 30:28–30, my translation)

As for doing or not doing "work" on the Sabbath, Christ himself famously continued also on Sabbath days to do his "work" of healing, of bringing new life to the previously lifeless and incapacitated (e.g., the man who had been paralyzed for thirty-eight years at the pool of Bethesda in John 5:1–18; the woman who had been bent over for eighteen years in Luke 13:10–17), of bringing light where previously there was darkness (as to the man born blind in John 9). He did this much to the chagrin of the Jewish religious authorities of his time, who seemed to think that God's work, of bringing life from death and light from darkness, ceased on the seventh day. Jesus explains to them that his Father's "rest" on the seventh day did not mean God became inactive: "My Father has been working until now," says Jesus on a Sabbath day, "and I have been working" (John 5:17 NKJV). And indeed Christ "worked" even on Holy and Great Saturday, when he bodily "rested" in the tomb and at the same time was bringing life to those who had been awaiting him in Hades. In the Byzantine church calendar, the fact that God's ongoing "work" in our world means bringing life from death is accentuated also by celebrating the raising of Lazarus (John 11) on the preceding Saturday, the sixth Saturday of Lent that is known as "Lazarus Saturday."

Christianity takes on a divinized understanding of Sabbath "rest," which means "working" always to embrace and re-embrace the light-bringing and life-creating "work" of God, in faith and synergy with him. Christians are called to participate in the "work" and hence "rest" of the Creator, applying it not to work per se, but to all work that is divorced from faith or that is not in synergy with God. That is why, in the rite of Holy Baptism during the first anointing (with the Oil of Gladness), the celebrant anoints the hands of the one to be baptized, saying a psalm verse that refers to God's hands: "*Your hands have made and fashioned me*" (Pss 117/118:73a) Henceforth the work of the hands of the Christian is to spring from faith in our Creator's ceaseless "work" in our midst, as we put to "rest" our fears of financial insecurity, human opinion, and other God-less fears. By replacing fear with faith on a daily basis, we enter into God's rest (cf. Ps 95:7–11), as the author of Hebrews explains: "*There remains therefore a rest for the people of God. For he who has entered His rest has himself also ceased from his works as God did from His. Let us therefore be diligent to enter that rest*" (Heb 4:9–11a NKJV). We are to be "diligent" to enter that rest, because faith takes work. It takes work to nourish our faith daily, and not to slip into the self-centered (rather than God-centered) motivations and resulting fears that motivate God-less kinds of activity. Thus, our Lord tells us directly that faith in him is "*the* work of God" that we have cut out for us: "*Then they said to Him, 'What shall we do, that we may work the works of God?' Jesus answered and said to them, 'This is the work of God, that you believe in Him whom He sent*'" (John 6:28–29 NKJV).

The Sabbath Commandment Today

Does this mean that Christians do *not* need to rest, also physically? Does it mean that the God of the Old Testament, who created night and day, who cared and even commanded that we and our dependents rest (at least once a week), and who so loved the world that he sent us his only begotten Son to give us "rest" (as quoted above), no longer cares whether we ever rest in the New Testament? No. In fact, Christ goes out of his way to remind that we, as human beings, need the Sabbath rest, when he points out that the Sabbath is "for" man, and not the other way around (Mark 2:27). The point of the Sabbath commandment was not to place additional, unnecessary burdens on human beings, as it did in the priestly traditions of post-exilic Judaism.[20] It was to be a blessing, not a burden. Christ also corrects our understanding and practice of the Sabbath

20. Rordorf, *Sunday*, 61–63.

commandment by reminding us of the freedom that we have in him, "the Son of man," who is "Lord even of the Sabbath" (Mark 2:28), to keep this commandment *as sons and daughters of man* in the freedom of his Spirit. It has been noted that the Aramaic word "barnasha" that is behind the Greek "*yios tou anthropou*" (son of man) could be translated as both "son of man" or simply, "man." In other words, one might dare translate Mark 2:28 as "Man is lord even of the Sabbath"![21]

In the era of the church we "keep holy" his Sabbath in different ways and *throughout our entire week*, with the help of our liturgical traditions that honor our times of day and night, of work and rest, as well as our days and seasons of fasting and of feasting, intermittently. Even while it is particularly challenging in our twenty-four-seven culture to "keep holy" our times of rest, it is for that reason particularly important that we do so, as part of our Christian ministry to ourselves and others to "redeem the time."

Saturdays in Byzantine Liturgical Tradition:
All Saints and All Deceased

In Byzantine liturgical tradition, as mentioned previously, Saturdays are marked both by the remembrance of Holy and Great Saturday, when Christ "rested" in the tomb, and by the remembrance of God's "rest" on the seventh day of creation. The latter memory, of God's "rest" after the good work of creating the world, makes every Saturday a joyous day in memory of and gratitude for creation. More will be said below on the joyous character of Saturdays.

The Kontakion hymn of Holy and Great Saturday underlines that this day is henceforth "most blessed" (not only because God initially "blessed" it on the seventh day, Gen 2:3a), but because on this day Christ "had fallen asleep":

> He who shut in the depths is beheld dead, wrapped in
> fine linen and spices. The Immortal One is laid in a tomb
> as a mortal man. The women have come to anoint Him
> with myrrh, weeping bitterly and crying: "This Sabbath

21. Rordorf, *Sunday*, 64.

is the most blessed, on which Christ has fallen asleep. He will rise on the third day!"

All Saints and all the faithful deceased are commemorated on Saturdays for this reason—Christ was among the deceased on a Saturday. Note that in the earliest centuries of church history, before "saints" were formally canonized or recognized as such, there was no clear distinction between "all saints" and "all departed." After all, we are not given to know God's judgment of each departed faithful and, for all we know, all the faithful departed are saints. So, to say that "all saints" or "all departed" are commemorated on Saturdays originally meant one and the same thing. And in the Early Church many of the departed "saints" were martyrs, not only commemorated but celebrated. Hence the Saturday hymnography of the Oktoechos, the Byzantine liturgical book that governs the weekday services, most often thematizes not all the saints in general but the Holy Martyrs specifically, reflecting ancient-Christian times when the deceased faithful were often martyrs.[22]

No Strict Fasting and the Eucharist on Saturdays

In Byzantine Orthodox tradition, Saturday is "special" in that it is always a semi-festal or joyous day, with the exception of Holy and Great Saturday immediately preceding Pascha or Easter Sunday. Liturgically speaking, Saturday is "special" in the sense that the Divine Liturgy may be celebrated on all Saturday mornings (except when it happens to be the eve of the greatest feasts of Pascha, Nativity, and Theophany, when—technically—the Divine Liturgy is celebrated in the evening or in connection with the evening service of Vespers). The Divine Liturgy is celebrated on Saturday mornings also during Lent, when as a rule it is not celebrated on weekdays.

Because of the joyous and eucharistic character of Saturdays, strict fasting is canonically prohibited on all Saturdays of the year, except Holy and Great Saturday. That is to say, even if it is a fasting season (Lent, Dormition Fast, Nativity Fast, or Apostles' Fast), strict fasting rules are mitigated on Saturdays within the fasting season.

22. Skaballanovich, *Tolkovyj Tipikon*, 68–70.

The earliest mention of the Christian custom of not fasting on Saturdays is found in an early-third-century (Montanist) work of Tertullian (+ca. 220), *On Fasting* 14. It later enters the canonical legislation of the Orthodox Church in the fourth-century Canon 64 of the Holy Apostles, and in Canon 55 of the Council at Trullo (AD 691/692) that also explicitly criticizes the Roman practice of fasting on Saturdays during Lent.[23]

The tradition of not fasting or "resting" from fasting on Saturdays arises also as a symbolic representation of God's "rest" on the seventh day. In other words, one symbolizes God's "rest" on the seventh day by "resting" from fasting. As stated in the *Apostolic Constitutions* (about AD 380), a late-fourth-century compilation of earlier church orders compiled at Antioch, the Sabbath should not be a day of fasting "since it is the day of rest after creation" (v. 20).[24] We are thus given to understand that *rest* is not compatible with *fasting*, which is a state not of rest but of heightened vigilance and watchfulness. Centuries later the Byzantine commentator Theodore Balsamon (+*post*-AD 1195) explains the Saturday prohibition of fasting along similar lines. In his comments on Canon 64 of the Holy Apostles, Balsamon says that this canon prohibits fasting on Sundays and Saturdays because: 1. Sunday we remember the "universal joy" of the Resurrection and of being "created again," and 2. "Saturday is the memory of creation."[25] Closer to our time, the Serbian Orthodox canonist of the late nineteenth and early twentieth century, Bishop Nikodim Milaš, stresses in his commentary on this canon that Saturday is a non-fasting day as an expression both of joy and of rest: "Christians considered it a day of joy (*dnyom*

---

23. Canon 55 of Trullanum: "Since we have learned that those living in the city of Rome fast on the Saturdays of the Holy Forty Days, contrary to the traditional ecclesiastical observance, it has seemed good to the holy synod that also in the Church of Rome the canon shall immovably be observed that says: If any cleric shall be found to fast on The Lord's Day or Saturday (except one only), he is to be deposed, and if he is a layman he shall be cut off." Agapis, *Rudder*, 354.

24. Grisbrooke, *Apostolic Constitutions*, 47.

25. *Pravila Svjatyh Apostol i Svjatyh Oteč*, 130.

radosti)," writes Milaš, "dedicated to the memory of the creation of the world and of God's rest."[26]

How Can We Pray on Saturdays?

On Saturdays one might pray not only privately, but by going to church and praying liturgically. Saturdays are churchgoing days in the Byzantine Rite, because on Saturday evenings there is either a "vigil" or at least Vespers (of Sunday) celebrated, and/or there may be a Divine Liturgy celebrated on Saturday morning as described above. While all Saturdays of the year are days of commemorating the deceased and all saints, several Saturdays of the year, known as "Memorial Saturdays" or "Saturdays of Souls," are dedicated to the commemoration of the deceased in an especially solemn manner, e.g., the second, third, and fourth Saturdays of Lent (in Russian Orthodox and related traditions), the Saturday before Pentecost Sunday, and several other Saturdays. Most church-parishes celebrate a Divine Liturgy on these Saturdays, and these services are usually well-attended.

As far as our private prayer on Saturdays goes, we might integrate brief prayers for the deceased and to all the saints into the hourly prayer discipline throughout our day, as well as psalm verses that celebrate God as Creator and re-affirm our vocation to "work" and "rest" in synergy with him. Whether we head for a church service on Saturday morning (and/or evening), or remain at home and simply rest from our weekday work schedule, and/or do our weekly laundry, housecleaning or garden work, or spend time with family or friends, we can try to remember to pray quietly to ourselves or aloud (if we are alone) throughout our Saturday:

- *"All Saints, pray to God for us!"*
- *"Give rest, O Lord, to the soul(s) of Your deceased servant(s) (N)!"*
- *"Your hands have made and fashioned me."* (Pss 117/118:73a)

---

26. Milaš, *Pravila Pravoslavnoj Čerkvi*, 141.

In the second prayer, we can insert the name or names of specific deceased, for whom we want to pray. We might also visit a cemetery on Saturdays, and place flowers or light a candle at the grave of a deceased loved one. Or we could place their photo near our icons at home, lighting an extra candle next to it, to help us remember our deceased in prayer on Saturdays. By praying to all the saints and for the deceased on Saturdays, we re-affirm our love for and communion with all the saints and departed. We also re-affirm our faith in life-after-death, in the common resurrection.

On Saturdays we might also be extra-attentive to praising God as Creator and for his creation, including all of us. It is a great day to take some time for a walk outdoors, to do some garden work if we have a garden, and—whatever we happen to be doing—to re-affirm our gratitude to God as Creator and for our dignifying vocation as responsible and responsive participants in his creation. In the brief "Saturday prayers" listed above, one might also include a verse from one of the psalms of the First Hour, "And let the brightness of the Lord our God be upon us" (Pss 89/90:19), which is useful every morning throughout our First Hour prayer as we begin our (work) day, but particularly appropriate on Saturdays.

SUNDAY

Sunday, the day of the Lord's resurrection from the dead, in English and many other languages is named after the sun, one of the seven "planets" of the pagan planetary week. As the planetary week came into use in the first to third centuries AD, the church adopted a Christianized sense of the "day of the sun" (*dies solis* in Latin), as the day Christ "rises" (as does the sun, *anatellein*) from death and darkness.[27] In Christian tradition Sunday is also known as the Lord's day, as in the Greek *Kyriaki* (from *kyriake hemera*, the Lord's day), and in the Romance languages (from the Latin *dies dominicus*) as in the French *dimanche*, the Italian *domenica*, Romanian *duminică*,

27. The Christian association of Christ's resurrection with the rising sun also led to the christianized sense of the Jewish custom of praying toward the East, and Christian churches were required to be "oriented" or to face East (Apostolic Constitutions II. 57. 3). Grisbrooke, *Apostolic Constitutions*, 13.

Spanish and Portuguese *domingo*, etc. In most Slavic languages, Sunday is called *nedelya/nedilya/niedziela* (e.g., in Old Slavonic, Serbian, Bulgarian, Ukrainian, Polish), meaning "day of not-doing," reflecting the understanding of Sunday as a day of rest. In Russian it is called *voskresenie*, meaning "resurrection." In Hebrew and Arabic, Sunday is "the first day" (*yom rishon, yom al-ahad*), while in Christian understanding it is both the first day and the eighth day, as will be explained below.

Sunday as the Lord's Day, the Day of the Lord's Supper

Early Christians called Sunday *the Lord's Day (kyriake hemera)* not primarily because the Lord rose from the dead on this day, but because Christians gathered as a community to celebrate *the Lord's Supper (kyriakon deipnon)* on this day.[28] It was the weekday when the risen Lord appeared to his disciples and broke bread or ate with them,—first, on the evening of the day of his resurrection, at Emmaus and then at the place where they were gathered, in the same room where he had accomplished his mystical or "last" supper with them (Luke 24:30–31; cf. John 20:19–23; and Mark 16:14); and a week later at that same place, when Thomas was with them (John 20:26–29). Sunday was also the day of Pentecost, when the Holy Spirit descended on the apostles and others gathered with them *in that same room*, filling and henceforth empowering the gathered church with the presence of the Lord, in and by his Holy Spirit. And it is this that made the Sunday Eucharist what it is thereafter: the encounter with the risen Lord through the Spirit that he bestows. Baptism was also a sacrament celebrated on Sundays by ancient Christians, as will be explained in our discussion of Sunday as "the eighth day" below.

Thus, even though Thursday was the weekday of the Lord's "last supper" with his disciples before his death, and perhaps of his "last supper" with them right before his ascension, which happened on a Thursday after he came together—perhaps for a meal—with them (*synalizomenos*, as it says in Acts 1:4), it was not the memory

---

28. Rordorf, *Sunday*, 221–30.

of these "last" Thursday supper(s) that became most important for the Eucharistic gatherings of Christians, but the joyous memory of his "first" Sunday-supper(s) with them after his resurrection. Note that the adjective *"kyriakos"* (meaning *the Lord's*) is used in the New Testament only in reference to these two, the Lord's Supper and the Lord's day: First, Saint Paul uses it in 1 Cor 11:20 in reference to the Lord's Supper, and later in Rev 1:10 we find the earliest mention of "the Lord's Day," or the day on which the author receives his revelation *en te kyriake hemera* (not to be confused with *hemera kyriou* or "the day of the Lord" that meant the last day). We find a similar expression in the contemporaneous (late-first-century or early-second-century) church order, the *Didache*, which instructs its community to gather for the Eucharist on this day: "On the Lord's own day (*kata kyriaken de kyriou*), assemble in common to break bread and give thanks" (*Did.* 14:1).

Sunday, then, was for the earliest Christians the day of gathering for worship, to celebrate the Eucharist. It was not, as mentioned in the previous section, the day of rest. As Willy Rordorf notes in his seminal work, *Sunday: The History of the Day of Rest and Worship in the Earliest Centuries of the Christian Church*, no one in the pre-Constantinian Roman Empire, neither Jews, Greeks, nor Romans, stopped work on Sundays. And Christians, many of whom were from the lower strata of society, could not possibly stop work on Sundays, nor were they aware of any commandment to do so. By resting on Sundays, they also would have risked revealing themselves as Christians, hence in the early church communal Sunday worship happened very early in the morning and/or after supper in the evening.[29]

It was only after Emperor Constantine's legislation concerning Sundays (from AD 321)[30] that church authorities gradually be-

---

29. Rordorf, *Sunday*, 154–56.

30. Constantine's first law concerning Sunday was issued on March 4, 321. It stated that all workers should rest "on the most honorable day of Sunday," with the notable exception of farmers, who were allowed to work if they needed to. The exception of farmers from Constantine's Sunday law places it in stark contrast to the Old Testament Sabbath commandment, which expressly forbade agricultural work on the Sabbath. Cf. Rordorf, *Sunday*, 162.

gan also to legislate the "keeping holy" of Sundays, and eventually to equate the Sabbath rest to Sundays. This was not because the church was traditionally concerned with keeping the Sabbath rest in the Old Testament sense; it was rather in response to various un-Christian tendencies of the later-fourth-century. For example, Canon 29 of the Council of Laodicea (AD 363/364), which commands that Christians celebrate on Sundays and not on Saturdays, is aimed against "Judaizing" tendencies. Another concern of church leaders was idleness and un-Christian celebrations/amusements on Sundays.[31]

Sunday as the First and Eighth Day, and Day of Baptism

The Gospel accounts of the Lord's resurrection call Sunday by its Jewish name, "the first day (of the week)."[32] As the first day of the week, Sunday in Christian tradition reflects the theology of Day One of creation, on which the Spirit of God moved over the water, God created light, and separated the darkness from the light:

> In the beginning God made the heaven and the earth. But the earth was unsightly and unfurnished, and darkness was over the deep, and the Spirit of God moved over the water. And God said, Let there be light, and there was light. And God saw the light that it was good, and God divided between the light and the darkness. And God called the light Day, and the darkness he called Night, and there was evening and there was morning, one day. (Gen 1:1–5 LXX)

The Christian understanding of Sunday, enlightened by the Lord's emergence from the tomb on this day, enlightens also our understanding of the "one day" (*hemera mia*, LXX) at the beginning of creation. In the book of Genesis it is not called "the first day" but "one day," differently from the other days of creation, because there were as yet no other "days" and it stands alone, outside

31. Rordorf, *Sunday*, 168–71.

32. The women came to his tomb very early on "*te mia ton savvaton*," "*prote savvatou*," "*eis mian savvaton*," etc. (Mark 16:2, 9; Matt 28:1; Luke 24:1; John 20:1).

of any sequence and outside of any time. Hence early Christians (by the second century) called Sunday also "the eighth day," as a day that signified eternity, as one that was beyond the seven-day week. The idea about an "eighth day" existed already in ancient Judaism, as a name for the future eon.[33] In the Christian sense, however, "the eighth day" was not only in the future; it breaks into the here and now of church life, particularly in the sacraments, and particularly in the living memory of the Lord's resurrection and enduring presence among us on Sundays. This here-and-now of Pascha Sunday (and hence every Sunday) is emphatically proclaimed in the *Prokeimenon* (a psalm verse chanted several times before the Epistle) of the Byzantine Divine Liturgy on Pascha Sunday: "*This is the day that the Lord has made; let us rejoice and be glad therein*" (Pss 117/118:24).

The understanding of Sunday as "the eighth day" was connected in ancient Christianity to the celebration of baptism on Sundays,[34] particularly on Pascha or the Easter vigil.[35] For this reason, baptismal fonts and baptisteries in the Christian West (particularly in France and Italy) were octagonal or eight-sided in form.[36] The celebration of baptism on "the eighth day," i.e., on a Sunday, underscores the typological connection of baptism with "old covenants" between God and his people, most famously the one established with Abraham and involving circumcision, which also was done on an eighth day, specifically on the eighth day after the birth of a male child. All the "old covenants," the one with Noah, and the ones with Abraham and with Moses on Sinai, were celebrated in a strand of Second Temple Judaism on a Sunday, at the Festival of Weeks that fell on a Sunday, according to Qumran's *Book of Jubilees*. According to this pre-Christian text, all these covenants were established on the first day or on a Sunday.[37] The covenant with Noah was considered to have been established with all creation, because

---

33. Rordorf, *Sunday*, 48–49, 276.

34. Johnson, *Christian Initiation*, 85; Rordorf, *Sunday*, 254–71.

35. Bertonière, *Easter Vigil*, 65–66, 121; Johnson, *Christian Initiation*, 64, 122.

36. Stauffer, *Baptismal Fonts*, 22.

37. Osborne, *Cosmic Liturgy*, 16–19.

Noah was told, as was Adam, to "increase and become numerous on the earth" (Gen 9:1); thus Noah replaced Adam as "the father of all creation." Saint Peter in both his epistles accentuates the symbolism of the "eight souls" (including Noah) "saved through water" in the flood (1 Pet 3:20–21; cf. 2 Pet 2:5) and connects that water with that of baptism: "And this water symbolizes the baptism that now saves you also" (1 Pet 3:21a NKJV). The covenants with Abraham and Moses were considered "renewals" of the "eternal" covenant with Noah, albeit limited to the descendants of Abraham.

Let us say a bit more about the covenant with Abraham, involving the somewhat bizarre, to some minds, rite of circumcision. It is important in the big picture of salvation history, in its typological connection to baptism, and yet is rarely contemplated or explained in modern-day catechetical instruction. How is circumcision *typologically connected* to baptism? Circumcision was "a sign of the covenant" (*en semeio diathekes*, Gen 17:11, LXX) between God and Abraham and his descendants; it was in those times a sign of belonging to God as his people. Hence the rite of circumcision was the "sign" of a covenant between God and his people, and a "rite of passage" therein. Yet it was but a foreshadowing of the New Covenant's "sign" and "rite of passage," baptism, which was to be instituted by the *passage* or *Pascha* of the Lord, from his death to his new life in the resurrection. Because circumcision was exclusive to males of one specific blood lineage—descended from Abraham—it may seem at first glance to have somehow elevated male procreative capacities to the central "sign" of being God's people. But in stark contrast to pagan cultures that idolize lingams, obelisks, and other phallic symbols, circumcision symbolically (and literally) cuts down a notch the male flesh, foreshadowing the "putting off the body of the flesh, by the circumcision of Christ" (Col 2:11b NKJV) that was to come in the New Covenant, accomplished by Jesus Christ, incarnate not of any man but of the Holy Spirit and the Virgin Mary.

In the New Covenant, accomplished by the death and resurrection of Christ and sealed by the gift of the Holy Spirit at Pentecost, baptism or *immersion* into the death and new life of Christ became the new "rite of passage" into the new people of God, not just for males but also females, and not just for Abraham's descendants but for all who embrace "the power to become children of God," and "who believe in His name: who were born, not of blood, nor of the will of the flesh, nor of the will of man, but of God" (John 1:12–13). Baptism has become "the circumcision made without hands," as Saint Paul explains in Col 2:9–14:

> For in him (Christ) the whole fulness of deity dwells bodily, and you have come to fulness of life in him, who is the head of all rule and authority. In him also you were circumcised with a circumcision made without hands, by putting off the body of flesh in the circumcision of Christ; and you were buried with him in baptism, in which you were also raised with him through faith in the working of God, who raised him from the dead. And you, who were dead in trespasses and the uncircumcision of your flesh, God made alive together with him, having forgiven us all our trespasses, having canceled the bond which stood against us with its legal demands; this he set aside, nailing it to the cross. (RSV)

Every Sunday, then, as we gratefully celebrate the New Covenant in Christ's blood (Luke 22:20) at the Eucharist, giving thanks for Christ's victory over death, we give thanks also for our passage into his life-bringing New Covenant at baptism; for the "sign" and "seal" of the gift of the Holy Spirit that has marked us as belonging to his one body, the church, and continues to gather us as one people in him. We also can be said to *renew* our baptism at the Eucharist, because we offer ourselves and our gifts of bread and wine to be consecrated by the Holy Spirit, who re-presents us to Christ as his children, and re-presents him to us in the flesh in his body and blood. This "Pentecost event" that happens every Sunday at the Divine Liturgy recalls both Pentecost Sunday, when the Holy Spirit descended on the apostles, and the very beginning of creation, when on Day One the Spirit of God moved over the water and darkness (as a hen brooding over her eggs), until light came forth from the darkness by God's word (Gen 1:1–3). The God who commanded light to shine out of darkness on Day One is the same God we celebrate every Sunday, the day on which his Son came forth from a dark tomb "clothed in majesty/beauty (*evprepeia*)," in the "new" light of the resurrection. In the words of Saint Paul: "For it is the God who commanded light to shine out of darkness, who has shone in our hearts to *give* the light of the knowledge of the glory of God in the face of Jesus Christ" (2 Cor 4:6 NKJV). When the Son of God emerges by the power of his divinity "in majesty/beauty" from the dark tomb on a Sunday, he reveals himself to be the Source of Light from the beginning, of the light that shone from darkness on Day One of creation. But the "new," uncreated light of the risen Lord is *more* than the light created on Day One. This "new" light, because it has shone from the God Man, can now "shine in our hearts" as no created light does, enlightening us with "the light of knowledge" when we allow ourselves to be divinized in communion with him.

All of the above themes of Sunday (resurrection, Eucharist, Pentecost, baptism, circumcision, creation) can be summarized as one theme: true life and light coming from the previously dead and dark, by the power of God.

Standing for Prayer on Sundays

There is an ancient Christian custom of not kneeling but standing for prayer on Sundays and throughout the entire Paschal season, from Pascha to Pentecost. Tertullian (+220) mentions it as one of the "unwritten" Christian customs in *The Chaplet* 3: "We count fasting or kneeling in worship on the Lord's Day to be unlawful. We rejoice in the same privilege also from Easter to Pentecost." Saint Peter of Alexandria (+311) also mentions it in the later third century (cf. Canon 15 of Saint Peter of Alexandria).

In our day, one might observe that in some churches both in East and West the celebrating clergy and people do kneel at certain points of Sunday liturgy. Contrary to this still-popular custom, the twentieth canon of the First Ecumenical Council of Nicea (AD 325) made not-kneeling on the Lord's day (and from Pascha to Pentecost) obligatory for all churches: "Forasmuch as there are certain persons who kneel on the Lord's Day and in the days of Pentecost, therefore, to the intent that all things may be uniformly observed everywhere (in every parish), it seems good to the holy Synod that prayer be made to God standing."

Why are we not to kneel on Sundays? Saint Basil the Great (+378) explains that by standing upright on Sundays, rather than kneeling, we symbolize or re-present with our own bodies the bodily resurrection of the Lord, our having risen from the dead together with him, and seeking "the things above" (*On the Holy Spirit* 27, cf. Canon 91 of Saint Basil the Great). Thus the "kneeling prayers" of Pentecost Sunday, attributed to Saint Basil, are not read at the vigil or Vespers or Matins of Pentecost Sunday, but at Vespers of the following day, Pentecost Monday, so as to avoid kneeling on Sunday. Even while for practical reasons this Vespers service, with the kneeling prayers of Pentecost Monday, is usually celebrated immediately after Divine Liturgy on Pentecost Sunday, the liturgical tradition is bending over backwards (or forwards, in this case) to avoid kneeling on a Sunday by placing the kneeling prayers outside the liturgical cycle of Pentecost Sunday and within Vespers of the next day.

Going to Church on Sundays

On Sundays we go to church and participate in the Divine Liturgy (or Mass), and in the preceding Sunday services of Vespers and Matins/Orthros (or the "All-Night Vigil" in Slavic traditions), if that is possible. Why? Because it is this dignifying and empowering thing that Christians have done on Sundays, whenever it was at all possible for them, ever since the risen Lord opened the Scriptures and broke bread with them on Day One of his resurrection, as described above.

But many baptized Christians do not go to church, because they can't or do not want to. First, let's talk about those who can't go to church, even though they would like to: Some people might hold a job that involves working on Sundays; they might live in a place with no church in their vicinity; they might be bedridden or caring for someone bedridden twenty-four-seven; they might be imprisoned with no access to a church; they might be married to someone who prevents them from going to church, or live in a land where it is illegal to go to their church, or where their church authorities have in some way become dangerous, for example, because these church authorities ally themselves too closely with an anti-Christian government. To these people, who do not go to church on Sundays for reasons beyond their control, I would suggest praying the Hours on Sundays as described in the section below, "Private Prayer on Sundays," if they can manage it. And I would remind them that nothing and nobody can separate us from the love of Christ, as Saint Paul says:

> Who shall separate us from the love of Christ? *Shall* tribulation, or distress, or persecution, or famine, or nakedness, or peril, or sword? As it is written: "For Your sake we are killed all day long; We are accounted as sheep for the slaughter." Yet in all these things we are more than conquerors through him who loved us. For I am persuaded that neither death nor life, nor angels nor principalities nor powers, nor things present nor things to come, nor height nor depth, nor any other created thing, shall be able to separate us from the love of God which is in Christ Jesus our Lord. (Rom 8:35–39 NKJV)

Next, let's talk about the many of us in our day who do not go to church, even when and where we easily could, but we "don't get it" or feel we get nothing out of it. Many of us say, "I am spiritual, but not religious," and don't go to church at all, because going to church means for us being "religious, but not spiritual." While I do not presume to know what is right for any reader, who prefers to abstain from churchgoing at this point in his or her life, because I believe we all, as adults in our church, should make our own responsible decisions, I would like to offer some thoughts about churchgoing, which may not have occurred to those of us who may have dismissed it without giving it much thought. Here are some thoughts on the positive aspects of going to church, for anyone who has not considered these.

If we have stopped going to church at this point in our lives because "we don't get it," or perhaps feel we get nothing out of it, we might consider the fact that we fortify and help *not only ourselves but others*, by "suiting up and showing up," and lending our voices to the big "thank you" to God that is liturgy. Here is how the Syriac *Didascalia Apostolorum*, a church order of the first half of the third century, instructs the bishop to induce his people to come to church:

> Now when you teach, command and warn the people to be constant in assembling in the Church, and not to withdraw themselves but always to assemble, lest any man diminish the Church by not assembling, and cause the body of Christ to be short of a member. For let not a man take thought of others only, but of himself as well, hearkening to that which our Lord said: *Everyone that gathereth not with me, scattereth* [Matt 12:30]. Since therefore you are the members of Christ, do not scatter yourselves from the Church by not assembling. Seeing that you have Christ for your head, as He promised— for you are partakers with us—be not then neglectful of yourselves, and deprive not our Saviour of His members, and do not rend and scatter His body. And make not your worldly affairs of more account than the word of God; but on the Lord's day leave everything and run eagerly to your Church; for she is your glory. (*Did. apost.* 13)

Here is another thought, not from the third century, but from my experience in our Internet age. In our divisive time of twenty-four-seven social media, when anger and fear often play a prominent role in our online-"communities," the Liturgy offers us a break from all that, as "a sacrifice of praise." We come and offer our thank you, "sacrificing" or setting aside "every worldly care," political or financial or otherwise. The Eucharist in both East and West is a "sacri-fice" (from the Latin words *sacer* and *facere*, meaning "making holy") that "makes holy" us and the gifts we offer before God as church, not by focusing on all that is wrong with the world, but by praising God for everything and everyone. Together we are lifted up and dignified to offer "a sacrifice of praise" as our communal self-offering, our laying aside of our merely-human communal "self," in response to the self-offering of Christ. At the Eucharist we even become "icons of the Cherubim," joining them in unconditional love of God, in response to his unconditional love for us. As we sing at Byzantine Divine Liturgy, in the Cherubic Hymn:

> We, who mystically represent (*mystikos eikonizontes,*
> *mystically are icons of*) the Cherubim,
> And chant the thrice-holy hymn to the Life-giving Trinity,
> Let us set aside every worldly care
> That we may receive the King of all,
> Who comes invisibly escorted by the Divine Hosts.

As distinct from the sort of "anti-church" that is "online community," which scatters our attention onto everything and everyone with the opinions and information they present to us twenty-four-seven in a disordered sort of fireworks display of these, real-life church brings us together into the specific praise of the life-giving Trinity, ordered within the specific time, place, and meaning of the liturgical celebration. Real-time Christian worship reorients us toward the meaning or "Logos" Who is Christ in our midst, and toward the specific occasion because of which we have gathered, which is the Sunday (Christ's resurrection) and the other commemorations (of a saint or feast) that are being celebrated on the same day. We *celebrate*, which means, we "come together to honor" the specific stories of the feast day (in the readings and liturgical hymns in honor of the resurrection and of the saint or feast), aligning ourselves and one another with God's truth, above and beyond the oft-disorienting and politicized unities we forge online.

Churchgoing also unifies and *straightens us out* physically. It not only aligns us mentally or "spiritually" with a certain set of sacred memories or ideas which we celebrate together, but it also, and perhaps even more importantly, makes us stand up and be counted, together with Christ and one another, in the same physical space and at the same time, in the celebration of the Eucharist. It is dignifying, nay, deifying, to offer ourselves into the real presence of Christ, and physically to partake of his body and blood at Holy Communion. It is also dignifying to offer ourselves physically into our church community, by "suiting up and showing up" for the Liturgy. Why? Because it takes at least a bit of discipline and courage, to get out of bed or off our couch on a Sunday morning, and "stand aright"

(*Orthoí* in Greek, as in the liturgical invitation, *Sophia, orthoí!* and *Prósti* in Slavonic, as in *Premudrost', prósti!*) among one another and in the presence of God and all the saints in church. To *stand aright* (*Orthoí* in Greek, as I already said) and worship is a vital aspect of being "*Ortho*-dox," which can be translated as "(up)right worship." Some readers might be skeptical about this definition of "Orthodox," if they underestimate the importance of standing up straight, not only in church but wherever and whenever we bear witness to Christ. But it is important, and in this point I wholeheartedly agree with the famous clinical psychologist Jordan Peterson, who in his *12 Rules for Life* lists this as his very first *rule*: "Stand up straight with your shoulders back."[38] My point is to suggest to those of us who see ourselves as "spiritual, not religious," that by participating in liturgy physically, we might also benefit spiritually.

Private Prayer on Sundays

On Sundays we also continue our hourly prayers of the First, Third, Sixth and Ninth Hours. Each of these Hours acquires special significance on The Lord's Day: The First Hour, as a celebration of "Christ, the true light," on a Sunday becomes a celebration focused on his light coming from the tomb in the early morning on this day. The time of the Third Hour, always a celebration of the Pentecost event that happened on a Sunday, on Sundays is celebrated sacramentally at the "Pentecost event" that is the Eucharist, when the Holy Spirit descends upon us and upon the gifts of bread and wine. The Divine Liturgy is usually celebrated at the time of the Third Hour, at some point between 9 am and midday (in which context the Russian Orthodox insertion of the Troparion of the Third Hour into the Eucharistic Prayer makes some "sense," I might add). In Western liturgical traditions, the Third Hour or the hour of "Terce" was traditionally that of the Mass on feast days, so it was called "*hora aurea*" or "*hora sacra*." The Sixth and Ninth Hours, as celebrations of the Lord's crucifixion and death, proclaim the Paschal Mystery that is celebrated with extra solemnity every Sunday.

38. Peterson, *12 Rules*, 1–28.

These Hours are either not celebrated at all in parish churches, or their celebration is misplaced to times of day/evening not traditional to them, as described in previous sections of this book. In Russian Orthodox tradition, the First Hour is usually chanted in abbreviated form quite late in the evening, at the end of what is called (but is not) "All-Night Vigil." Here it makes no sense, and the few people who are in church use this time to venerate the icons, go to confession, or to do something else, other than praying the First Hour of the day in the late evening. The Third and Sixth Hours, if chanted at all, are chanted immediately before the Divine Liturgy, when even the celebrating priest is doing something else, e.g., celebrating the Proskomide/Prothesis or hearing confessions. The Ninth Hour is not chanted in parish-churches, except on certain weekdays of Lent.

So, we could pray these Hours on Sundays more or less as we do on other days, whether or not we are able to go to church. From the moment we wake up in the morning, we can pray to ourselves or aloud the Troparion of the First Hour, "*In the morning hear my voice, my King and my God*," inserting between repetitions of the Troparion Sunday verses or prayers listed below. This is a warm-up for our more formalized morning prayers, if we do more formalized morning prayers and/or read the Prayers Before Holy Communion, and/or read the Scripture readings of the day.

A few more words about our preparation for Holy Communion: Whatever we pray privately, in preparation for Holy Communion, let us remember that our main "prayers before Holy Communion" are those of the Eucharistic celebration itself, along with the liturgical prayer and fasting that precedes it (i.e., the Vespers, Matins, Hours 1 and 3, and the morning fasting before the Eucharist). The Divine Liturgy itself is meant to be our main preparation for Holy Communion or our "mystagogy," the *leading us into the Mystery* of Holy Communion. If we are not well-versed in the texts and meanings of the Liturgy, we might take some time, perhaps on Sunday mornings before church, to read these texts and learn about them.[39]

39. Available on YouTube is my forty-seven-video course on each of the liturgical units of Byzantine Divine Liturgy, from "Blessed is the Kingdom"

From 9 am we might be either on our way to church or in church, praying the Third Hour if it is chanted in our parish. If we can't be in church, we pray the Troparion of the Third Hour (with Sunday-verses) and do likewise at the Sixth and Ninth Hours of our Sunday.

Below are some brief verses and prayers we could insert into our hourly prayers, in between the Troparion of each Hour, on Sundays. These thematize the leitmotifs of Byzantine-Rite Sundays— the cross and resurrection, the Lord's Supper, the saint(s) of the day, and the Theotokos. We pray to the Theotokos every day, but with extra focus on Sundays, because she is the primary witness to the cross and resurrection, exemplifying the praying, mother church:

- *"Glory be, O Lord, to Your holy Resurrection!"*
- *"Glory be, O Lord, to Your honorable Cross and Resurrection!"*
- *"Your own of Your own we offer to You, in all and for all."*
- *"Of Your mystical supper, O Son of God, accept me today as a communicant; for I will not speak of Your mystery to Your enemies, neither like Judas will I give You a kiss; but like the thief will I confess You: Remember me, O Lord, in Your kingdom."*
- *"Most Holy Theotokos, save us!"*
- *"Holy Martyr/Father/Mother N* (saint of the day), *pray to God for us!"*

---

to the end of the Anaphora. Search on YouTube for "Intro to Divine Liturgy Sister Vassa" or watch the first video (and access the full playlist of the rest of the videos) here: https://www.youtube.com/watch?v=WwSWPqB2Fgc&t=1s.

Table 2: Themes and Prayers of the Seven Days of the Week

Day	Theme(s)	Prayers
Monday	Angels	*Holy Archangels and Angels,* *pray to God for us!*
Tuesday	Saint John the Baptist	*Holy and great John, Forerunner of the* *Lord, pray to God for us!*
Wednesday	Cross, Theotokos	*Glory be, O Lord, to Your honorable Cross!* *Most holy Theotokos, save us!*
Thursday	Apostles, Saint Nicholas	*Holy Apostles, pray to God for us!* *Holy father Nicholas, pray to God for us!*
Friday	Cross, Theotokos	*Glory be, O Lord, to Your honorable Cross!* *Most holy Theotokos, save us!*
Saturday	All Saints, the deceased	*All Saints, pray to God for us!* *Give rest, O Lord, to the soul(s) of Your* *deceased servant(s) (N)!*
Sunday	Resurrection	*Glory be, O Lord, to Your holy Resurrection!* *Glory be, O Lord, to Your honorable Cross* *and Resurrection!*

3

Conclusions

IN THE INTRODUCTION TO this book, I mentioned the fear of being "scattered," which motivated the builders of the city and Tower of Babel. They undertook their building project because "otherwise," as they said, "we shall be scattered abroad upon the face of the whole earth" (Gen 11:4b NKJV). In other words, they feared ending up alone, each one scattered apart from the others throughout the earth. Their undertaking, based on self-centered fear rather than God-centered faith, turned their fear into a self-fulfilling prophecy, when they indeed "scattered abroad upon the face of the whole earth." This story is reminiscent of our modern-day predicament, in which our fear of being alone leads us to seek constant community via social media, which in effect scatters us "abroad" or into the "everywhere" of virtual reality, making us lonely all the more. It makes us lonely even in the midst of others in our homes, when we tap away at our phones at the breakfast table, in our beds, at dinner parties, etc., often oblivious to those in our physical presence.

By way of conclusion, I will reflect on how praying the hours and days helps us to rediscover the God-given remedy to our "scatteredness" and fear thereof. This remedy is known as "church." The Kontakion hymn of the feast of Pentecost, which is known as "the birthday of the church," compares the division of the tongues at Babel with the call to unity through the fiery tongues of Pentecost:

When the Most High came down and confused the
tongues, He divided the nations; but when He distrib-
uted the tongues of fire, He called all to unity. Therefore,
with one voice, we glorify the All-holy Spirit!

In a mystical sense, the church is the sacrament/mystery of
unity, and in the historical sense it is God's building project, on
which human beings are called to work in synergy with him, according to God's house-building rules or "*oikonomia.*" The Wisdom
of God, our Lord Jesus Christ, has already laid the foundation of
his "house," offering himself as its cornerstone. He also established
the "seven pillars" of his "house" that are the seven days of the week
or time, thanks to which the church continues to develop and to
do its transfiguring work, of leading us from death to new life. In
what follows I will reflect on how the daily and hourly discipline of
traditional prayer informs and deepens our understanding of what
it means to be church within time.

Being Church in the Now

Praying the hours and days attentively and according to church-tradition helps us to be present to our "now," to each hour and day, as
church. Even while we "remember" certain moments from the past,
from salvation history, throughout our prayer discipline, we honor
and enlighten our "now" by praising God for his salvific works in
the context of this "now." The sacred memories of biblical tradition
do not drag us into living in the past, because they remain relevant
to God's eschatological purpose, toward which each one of us is
being nudged on our road to salvation, Hour after Hour and from
day to day. The prayers of the Hours help us to relate biblical events
to our own lives, as in the Third-Hour Troparion, which relates the
descent of the Holy Spirit onto the apostles at Pentecost to our own
need for the renewal of the Holy Spirit within us.

Our "now" is thus expanded, becoming connected to our
biblical past, and directing us forward into the future eschaton or
fulfilment. The primary focus remains "now," as in the common
ending of Byzantine doxologies: "*Both now and ever, and unto the*

ages of ages." The "now" is our immediate focus, but it is not unconnected to the past and future, so we do not get caught up in "the tyranny of the present."

Being Church by Praying Traditionally

Thus, praying the hours and days "traditionally," according to the meanings attached to the hours and days in an ancient church tradition, fosters our sense of belonging to something bigger than ourselves. We did not make it up ourselves; it is a gift largely ignored by us today, but still available to us and passed on from over a millennium ago, utilized by many generations of "redeemers of the time," more specifically of redeemers of different "times," who prayed this prayer tradition in different settings and historical circumstances. Past generations did not all pray this prayer tradition in the exact same way, even while the theological meanings and memories attached to the Days and Hours, along with some of the psalms and prayers of the Hours, have remained constant for over a millennium.

Consequently, praying "traditionally" does not mean praying exactly as Christians did in some past century. To live tradition does not mean simply to repeat it, in a way that is uncreative and divorced from life. But this seems to be our approach to the Liturgy of the Hours; we usually have a very small minority of the faithful chant or attend these services (Vespers, Matins, and the Little Hours), often chanted not at their proper liturgical times, if these services are chanted at all, while most parishioners only show up for Divine Liturgy. Try as we might, it is not possible for us to pray exactly as did Christians in some past century, especially when it comes to the Liturgy of the Hours, because of the changes we have experienced in our perception of time. We experience time differently from ancient Christians, because of the transition from the sundial to the mechanical clock. We also experience time differently from Christians of just a decade ago, because of the advent of twenty-four-seven Internet time and our attachment to mobile phones.

Nonetheless, our Christian vocation to "redeem the time" has not gone anywhere; it has only become more urgent in the unredeemed wilderness of twenty-four-seven Internet time. We should not be wandering through this wilderness alone and unarmed, or not sufficiently armed. To my mind, we do not primarily need the Prayer Book, or its Morning and Evening Prayers that focus mostly on our individual sins. We need to bring out "the big guns" of our Tradition for taming the beasts in this wilderness. That is to say, we need the Liturgy of Time, with its depth of theology and biblical memories, beginning with creation and extending forward, into the life of the age to come. We can walk our cross-carrying journeys in a more theologically and ecclesiologically mindful manner, by living the prayer tradition of the hours and days as we can, realistically adapting it to our present-day circumstances rather than being trapped in their disorienting chaos.

The Goodness of Church Time

Time is a good thing, from the Christian point of view, as we discover when we "redeem" each hour and day by participating in the traditional Liturgy of Time. We need not wake up in the morning with a feeling of dread, or of existential angst, as many of us might in our time, for no particular reason. As we become "redeemers of the time," we "accept" it as did our Redeemer, when he "proclaimed," in the words of Isaiah, "the acceptable year of the Lord" (Luke 4:19); we accept our "now" as did Saint Paul, when he exclaimed, "Behold, now is the accepted time; behold, now is the day of salvation" (2 Cor 6:2 NKJV). We also increasingly adopt the forward-looking and life-affirming attitude of the Nicene-Constantinopolitan Creed, at the end of which we profess: "I look for the resurrection of the dead, and the life of the age to come." When we consistently direct our hearts to God, throughout our ups and downs, we allow his presence to liberate us from the kind of existential angst that comes from approaching each day in self-reliance, as if we carry the burdens of the whole world on our own shoulders. Even if we wake up in this state of mind, we can immediately arm ourselves with the First-Hour Troparion and reconnect with God, saying, "In the morning hear my voice, my King and my God!" It works. It lifts us out of the rut of fear, and into the light of faith, whenever we make that decision to let God into our day, rather than remaining in self-isolated fear.

Redeeming the Time as Dignifying Work

The daily and hourly work of "redeeming the time" is dignifying, not only because it is important work, of laypeople and clergy alike, but because we make our own decision to do it. We also determine how we do it, either more or less intensely, just once each "Hour" or more often, with or without the insertion of psalm verses or other prayers, quietly or aloud, etc. We accept responsibility for our own prayer schedule, as hired hands in a church enterprise that is called "Redeeming the Time." We are not the only ones working at this enterprise; we are not alone, but lending our voices to the great choir that is the praying church, the royal priesthood, offering a daily and hourly "sacrifice of praise."

Being Church within Time

When we become prayerfully attentive to each Hour and Day, rather than letting these slip our minds as does sand through an hourglass, we become more awake to the fact of church-being within time, and of our being church within time. This may seem obvious, but it merits more ecclesiological reflection in our day, when many tend to see "church" and its "tradition" as timeless and hence unchangeable.

"Church" is not an unchangeable abstract, although it does involve unchangeable or timeless "mysteries," which are the aspects of God's Being that are not visible to us. Throughout history and within the time of each of our earthly lives, God offers us glimpses or insights into his timeless mysteries, through the "mystagogy" (or "introduction into the mysteries") of the sacraments of the church, and of our everyday cross-carrying journey. The *ways and means* by which we receive, pass on, and celebrate the mysteries are not time-less, meaning that they change. I.e., our language evolves, as do our translations of biblical, liturgical, and other theological texts; our liturgical rites and the architecture of our church buildings change, as do church vestments and music; the types of ministries and roles we take on as church members within a specific culture or historical context change; the technologies we employ to receive and teach catechetical instruction develop, etc.

Neither "church" nor "tradition" is unchangeable, even though we as church people are often resistant to change that which needs changing in church tradition. An important example both of the changeability of church tradition and of our reluctance to change it is the brokenness of the Liturgy of the Hours in the Orthodox Church, already for many centuries. The good news is that we can begin mending this broken instrument, which has ceased to work according to its original purpose, which is to help us "redeem the time" in which we live. We can change the way we put this instru-ment to work for us, so let us do that, because we have the time to do so.

Bibliography

ABC News. "Mark Zuckerberg Harvard Commencement Speech 2017 FACEBOOK CEO'S FULL SPEECH." *YouTube*, May 26, 2017. https://www.youtube.com/watch?v=QM8l623AouM.

Agapius (Hieromonachus), Nikodemus. *The Rudder (Pedalion)*. Translated by D. Cummings. Chicago: The Orthodox Christian Educational Society, 1957.

Alexopoulos, Stefanos. "Anamnesis, Epiclesis, and Mimesis in the Minor Hours of the Byzantine Rite." *Worship* 94 (2020) 228–45.

Archdiocese of Canada, ed. *The Oktoechos or, The Book of Eight Tones*. Otego, NY: Octoechos of the Monastary of the Myrhhbearing Women, 1999. https://www.archdiocese.ca/content/complete-octoechos-book-eight-tones.

Athanasius. "Tolkovanija na psalmy." In *Tvorenija izhe vo svjatyh otza nashego Afanasija Velikago, Arhiepiskopa Aleksandrijskago*, edited by Svjato-Troitskaja Sergieva Lavra, 4:40–422. 4 vols. Sergiev Posad: Svjato-Troitskaja Sergieva Lavra, 1903.

Bertonière, Gabriel. *The Historical Development of the Easter Vigil and Related Services in the Greek Church*. Orientalia Christiana Analecta 193. Rome: Pont. Institutum Studiorum Orientalium, 1972.

Bradshaw, Paul F. *Daily Prayer in the Early Church*. London: Alcuin Club, 1981.

———. "Did Jesus Institute the Eucharist at the Last Supper?" In *Issues in Eucharistic Praying in East and West. Essays in Liturgical and Theological Analysis*, edited by Maxwell E. Johnson, 1–19. Collegeville: Liturgical, 2010.

———. *Two Ways of Praying: Introducing Liturgical Spirituality*. London: Abingdon, 1995.

———. "Cathedral vs. Monastery: The Only Alternatives for the Liturgy of the Hours?" In *Time and Community. In Honor of Thomas J. Talley*, edited by J. Neil Alexander, 123–36. NPM Studies in Church Music and Liturgy. Washington, DC: Pastoral, 1990.

Carr, Nicholas. *The Shallows: What the Internet Is Doing to Our Brains*. New York: Norton, 2011.

Chesterton, G. K. *Orthodoxy*. New York: Barnes & Noble, 2007.

Clément, Olivier. *Transfiguring Time: Understanding Time in the Light of the Orthodox Tradition*. Translated by Jeremy N. Ingpen. Hyde Park, NY: New City Press, 2019.

Colling, Egan P. *A Book of Hours: Meditations on the Traditional Hours of Christian Prayer*. Chesterton: Conciliar, 2010.

DB Business. "Elon Musk—Warning." *YouTube*, October 31, 2020. https://www.youtube.com/watch?v=lowpFm14rJc.

Goldhill, Simon. *The Christian Invention of Time: Temporality and the Literature of Late Antiquity*. Cambridge: Cambridge University Press, 2022.

Grisbrooke, W. Jardine, ed. and trans. *The Liturgical Portions of the Apostolic Constitutions: A Text for Students*. Alcuin/GROW Liturgical Study 13–14. Bramcote-Nottingham: Grove, 1990.

Guiver, George. *Company of Voices: Daily Prayer and the People of God*. New York: Pueblo, 1988.

Gumbrecht, Hans Ulrich. *Production of Presence: What Meaning Cannot Convey*. Stanford: Stanford University Press, 2004.

Heying, Heather, and Brett Weinstein. *A Hunter-Gatherer's Guide to the 21st Century*. New York: Portfolio, 2021.

John of Damascus. *Tochnoe izlozhenie pravoslavnoj very*. In *Polnoe sobranie tvorenij sv. Ioanna Damaskina*, edited by Peterburgskaja Duhovnaja Akademija, 1:157–345. 1 vol. St. Petersburg: St. Petersburg Theological Academy, 1913.

Johnson, Maxwell E. *The Rites of Christian Initiation: Their Evolution and Interpretation*. Collegeville: Liturgical, 1999.

Le Goff, Jacques. *Time, Work, and Culture in the Middle Ages*. Chicago: University of Chicago Press, 1980.

Manchester, Peter. *The Syntax of Time: The Phenomenology of Time in Greek Physics and Speculative Logic from Iamblichus to Anaximander*. Leiden-Boston: Brill, 2005.

Mateos, Juan. "L'office monastique à la fin du IVe siècle: Antioche, Palestine, Cappadoce." *Oriens Christianus* 47 (1963) 53–88.

———. "Un Horologion inédit de Saint-Sabas: Le codex sinaïtique grec 863 (IXe siècle)." In *Mélanges Eugène Tisserant*, 3.1:47–76. Studi e Testi 233. Vatican: Typis polyglottis Vaticanis, 1964.

Milaš, Nikodim. *Pravila Pravoslavnoj Čerkvi s tolkovanijami Nikodima*. Vol. 1, *Episkopa Dalmatinsko-Istrijskago*. St. Petersburg: Izdanie S. Peterburgskoj Duhovnoj Akademii, 1911.

Orthodox Church in America, ed. *Baptism*. N.p.: Orthodox Church in America, 2012. https://www.oca.org/files/PDF/Music/Baptism/baptism-service.pdf.

Osborne, Alfred. *A Cosmic Liturgy: Qumran's 364-Day Calendar*. Turnhout, Belg.: Brepols, 2019.

Peterson, Jordan. *12 Rules for Life: An Antidote to Chaos*. London: Penguin Random House, 2018.

Plank, Peter. *Phos hilaron: Christushymnus und Lichtdanksagung der frühen Christenheit*. Bonn, Germ.: Borengässer, 2001.

Pravila Svjatyh Apostol i Svjatyh Oteč s tolkovanijami. Moscow: Tipografija Sovremennyh Izvestij, 1876.

Rordorf, Willy. *Sunday: The History of the Day of Rest and Worship in the Earliest Centuries of the Christian Church.* Translated by A. A. K. Graham. Philadelphia: Westminster, 1968.

Scott-Macnab, David. "The Many Faces of the Noonday Demon." *Journal of Early Christian History* 8 (2018) 22–42.

Skaballanovich, Mikhail. *Tolkovyj Tipikon.* Kiev, Ukr.: Tipografia Akzionernago Obshchestva, 1910.

Stauffer, S. Anita. *On Baptismal Fonts: Ancient and Modern.* Alcuin/GROW Liturgical Study 29–30. Bramcote-Nottingham, UK: Grove, 1994.

Taft, Robert F. "The Divine Office: Monastic Choir, Prayer Book, or Liturgy of the People of God? An Evaluation of the New Liturgy of the Hours in its Historical Context." In *Beyond East and West: Problems in Liturgical Understanding,* 259–79. Second Revised and Enlarged Edition. Rome: Edizioni Orientalia Christiana Pontifical Oriental, 2001.

———. *The Liturgy of the Hours in East and West.* 2nd rev. ed. Collegeville: Liturgical, 1993.

Talley, Thomas J. *The Origins of the Liturgical Year.* 2nd amended ed. New York: Pueblo, 1991.

Ware, Kallistos. "Tradition and Creativity." *Sobornost* 42 (2020) 8–21.

Winkler, Gabriele. "Über die Kathedralvesper in den verschiedenen Riten des Ostens und Westens." *Archiv für Liturgiewissenschaft* 16 (1974) 53–102.